Michael Wilkinson and Richard Smith
Leadership Strategies – The Facilitation Company

CLICK

THE
VIRTUAL MEETINGS
BOOK

Northwest State Community College

From the #1 Provider of
Facilitation Training and Professional Facilitators

Published by Leadership Strategies Publishing
A division of Leadership Strategies—The Facilitation Company

56 Perimeter Center East, Suite 103
Atlanta, Georgia 30346
800-824-2850

www.leadstrat.com

Substantial discounts on bulk quantities are available to corporations, governments, non-profits, and other organizations. For details and discount information, contact Leadership Strategies at 800-824-2850.

Publisher's Cataloging-In-Publication Data
(Prepared by The Donohue Group, Inc.)

Wilkinson, Michael, 1957-
  CLICK : the virtual meetings book / Michael Wilkinson and Richard Smith. -- 1st ed.

  p. : ill. ; cm.

  Includes bibliographical references and index.
  ISBN: 978-0-9722458-5-2

  1. Computer conferencing. 2. Business meetings. 3. Communication in management. I. Smith, Richard (Richard W.), 1945- II. Title. III. Title: Virtual meetings book

HF5734.7 .W55 2013
658.4/56   2013912383

Manufactured in the United States of America
Cover design by Jelena Mirkovic
Interior design by redbat design

FIRST EDITION

*Dedicated to the field of facilitation,
which has been a blessing for our families
and a source of joy and professional
fulfillment for us. May this book advance
the field in this new virtual age.*

Table of Contents

Table of Contents

Table of Contents

Table of Contents

Table of Figures

Table of Figures

Acknowledgements

When we agreed to write this book on an accelerated schedule and make it our number-one priority for the second and third quarter of 2013, we thought we knew what we were getting ourselves into. With four prior books behind us, we thought we knew the effort it would take to bring this one into fruition. We thought we knew. As a project estimator once said, "Do your best job at estimating what it will take, and then double it, and you might be almost there."

We weren't even close! If not for the support of a few very special people, CLICK would not have, quite frankly, clicked.

Kris Casariego, the director of marketing at Leadership Strategies, has been tireless in her support of this work. From setting up initial interviews with virtual platform sellers to reviewing drafts and recommending revisions, Kris has been a true partner in bringing CLICK into creation.

To our project manager, Sandra Liburd, we want to say thank you for putting up with two impossible-to-manage bosses. We so appreciate your "C-ness"—that ability to get us focused on the details when our heads are way in the clouds.

Thank you, Sarah Cypher, the CEO at the Threepenny Editor, for your superb copyediting skills; and Kristin Summers, head of Redbat Design, for another superb layout. After our successful collaboration on *The Executive Guide to Facilitating Strategy*, working with the two of you again has been a pleasure.

To our cover designer, Jelena Mirkovic, we want to say thank you for an inspiring design that so well captures the CLICK message. You are truly gifted. Thanks also to Crowdspring. com for providing the platform for us to receive your design and 150 others through their crowdsourcing model.

We thank all the associates at Leadership Strategies who picked up the slack during this intense period. Together, the sales, marketing, facilitation, and operations teams continue to create and sustain trusted client relationships while delivering a level of service that has resulted in a world-class, 75-percent-plus net promoter score over the past several years. It's a joy to be part of the team.

To our customers who have allowed us to test our virtual meeting theories that have led to the insights that we are sharing with others through this book, we say thank you. We want especially to thank our friends at Citi and Manheim who have led the way in helping us to test the outer limits of virtual meetings and training.

Michael thanks his three favorite ladies: Danielle, my future journalism major who loves family, friends, and chocolate, but not necessarily in that order; Gabrielle, my scholar-athlete whose strong competitive drive is equally matched by a heart of gold—she will run you over on the soccer field and then reach back to help you up; and Sherry, my partner in business and my partner in life, whose laughter and joy thrill me every day.

Acknowledgements

Richard would like to thank all of the people who have helped him appreciate the art of facilitation—past, present, and future. Personally, the power of collaboration is an amazing tool for coming to decisions. Professionally, it is fascinating to observe how effective a group's power and wisdom can be when guided by a skilled facilitator, who is also a part of the group. In fact, largely, that is what running great virtual meetings is about: facilitating a group when you are a part of that group. And my gratitude also goes to my three favorite ladies: my wife, Sue, and daughters Laura and Amanda.

Michael Wilkinson and Richard Smith
Leadership Strategies – The Facilitation Company
Sharing the Power of Facilitation with the World™
August 2013

CLICK

THE
VIRTUAL MEETINGS
BOOK

Leadership Strategies
The Facilitation Company

Why Virtual? | **1**

- The Virtual Dilemma
- Virtual Meetings: On the Rise
- Virtual Meeting Skills: Far Behind
- Why Engagement Is Critical
- The Virtual Meetings Framework
- What This Book Will Do for You
- CASE STUDY: It's 4:00 a.m. Do You Know Where Your Facilitator Is?

The Virtual Dilemma

The vice president of human capital has asked you to lead a virtual, cross-functional task force of seven people who have been charged with redesigning the dreaded annual performance review process. With the exception of you and one other headquarters person, the five other members of the team are in different offices around the country.

You have successfully led two task forces in the past; but these both had team members who were all headquarters-based. Everyone was always in the same room. This is the first time you will be leading a virtual team. So you are wondering, "How will this change my process?" Of course, some differences are obvious.

- You know that, since most team members won't be in the same room, people won't be able to see each other unless you use some type of video conferencing tool.

- Since most members of the team are not familiar with one another, people won't necessarily recognize voices or know who is speaking, especially in the first few meetings.

- If people can't see one another, this also means that people may be tempted to multi-task and not stay focused on what is going on.

- Not having people in the same room also can mean that the team members won't be able to read one another's expressions and body language, and therefore won't "see" the nonverbal cues that tell us someone agrees, disagrees, or simply wants to speak next.

- Finally, in face-to-face meetings, you typically have presentations that everyone views. You use flip charts to record what people are saying. These vehicles help keep people focused because everyone can see what is getting documented. Without a screen sharing tool that allows everyone to see the same thing, the team could lose significant productivity as it can take longer to get the same amount of work done.

While these differences may be obvious, what about those differences that aren't as obvious? And with virtual meetings, what do you have to do differently to adjust to the virtual environment? In other words, you are worried about this all-important question:

What will be different and how will I have to be different?

Virtual Meetings: On the Rise

You don't have to look very far to see that virtual meetings are on a meteoric rise. In our own organization, as the leading provider of professional facilitators and facilitation training in the US, during the twelve months leading up to the publication of this book we facilitated more virtual meetings than in the prior five years combined. In fact, two months prior to the publication of this book, one of us facilitated a half-day, face-to-face session for a group in Atlanta and three half-day virtual sessions—two for a group in the UK and one for a group in Poland, *all in the same week*!

What's fueling the growth? We believe that a combination of several factors is providing both the means and the motivation.

Factors affecting growth in virtual meetings

- Access:
  Laptops, tablets, and smart phones with embedded webcams have become the norm. Before, to be "virtual ready," an organization needed a dedicated room with hardwired cameras and microphones; today people are participating in virtual meetings while sitting at their desk, driving their car, or standing in a grocery checkout line.

- Price:
  Advances in web-based technologies have brought into place easy-to-use tools at reasonable prices that make virtual communication available to large and small businesses alike. Further, the "freemium" model provides tools with basic features that people can use at no cost, while providing more advanced features for an additional fee.

- Need:
  As with nearly every business cycle, when the economy declines, travel budgets get cut drastically. Travel expenses for a monthly or quarterly team meeting are a luxury that many no longer can afford. "Flying someone in for a face-to-face" is often frowned upon. But in the most recent economic downturn, virtual meetings had become a viable option. The tools were available at a reasonable price. The access vehicles were becoming more universal. So when the need arose, there was a ready answer. People took it, and the meteoric rise began.

The acceleration to virtual is expected to continue, and to spread into new areas. According to Valerie Schreiner, vice president of product management and product development at Blackboard, the trend is moving away from formal calendar meetings: "The expansion seems to be in ad hoc, instant access types of meetings. Rather than rely on asynchronous communication to establish a synchronous meeting, if I can see you are available and initiate the conversation now, we can hold a virtual meeting right away." In addition, rather than existing as stand-alone systems, virtual meeting platforms are beginning to show up embedded in other applications such as customer relationship management systems and enterprise resource planning systems.

Virtual Meeting Skills: Far Behind

While the demand for virtual meetings is increasing, we can't say the same thing about the skill of meeting leaders who run these sessions. By nature, virtual meetings are more complex, require more planning to be highly effective, and must be executed in a different way to drive engagement, buy-in, and commitment to action.

Unfortunately, our experience has been that many meeting leaders actually do even *less* planning for a virtual meeting than they do for a face-to-face one. It's as if they believe that using technology and NOT having people in the same room combine to reduce the need for preparation. (It sounds ludicrous when you read it, doesn't it?)

In cases when a virtual meeting leader does recognize the need for preparation, the focus of preparation is on learning how to use the tool. Tool expertise is indeed critical. Can you imagine how painful it would be sitting through a face-to-face meeting where the meeting leader was learning how to use a flip chart marker? But preparing by just learning the tool is not enough. As Agnes Jozwiak, the brand manager of ClickMeeting, put it, "The priority should be on what you want to present, not on the tool you are presenting on."

What's the result of the lack of preparation and lack of skill in running virtual meetings? What we find are meetings that . . .

- don't start on time because people have difficulty with the technology,
- don't have key people present due to firewalls and other blockages,
- don't have a defined purpose due to lack of preparation,
- don't stay on topic because the meeting leader allows the meeting to wander,
- don't keep people engaged enough because people frequently multi-task since they aren't seen,
- don't address conflict because the leader often doesn't see the body language information that communicates silent disagreement, and
- don't deal with dysfunction because the meeting leader is distracted by the technology.

There are two fundamental issues with virtual meetings that meeting leaders must address to be consistently successful in achieving their desired outcomes.

The two fundamental issues with virtual meetings

- How will you ensure that every participant can access and proficiently perform within the virtual meeting environment?
- What are you going to do to keep people fully engaged who are not in the same room with you?

Why Engagement Is Critical

In face-to-face meetings, engagement is important. But in virtual meetings, engagement is critical. In face-to-face meetings, when engagement isn't happening, you, the meeting leader, can see it. You can see people who are working on their tablet, talking on the telephone, whispering to their neighbor, staring out the window at passersby, and even those who are taking a short nap. But this is rarely the case in virtual meetings. If you are holding a virtual meeting and don't have video, you could have meeting participants that are doing every behavior just described, and you might never know it—unless you are using engagement strategies that keep them focused and interacting. That's what this book is all about: using the art of facilitation to keep virtual meetings highly engaging and interactive.

The relationship between high engagement and better results couldn't be clearer, as shown in Figure 1.1, which demonstrates the two ways engagement leads to results.

Figure 1.1: The Engagement-to-Results Relationship

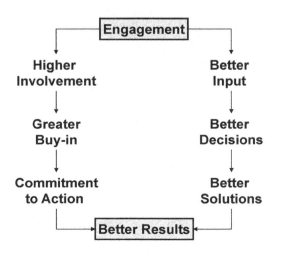

Through engagement you tend to get better input that leads to better decisions, better solutions, and better results. At the same time, when you engage participants, this tends to result in higher levels of involvement in discussions, which leads to greater buy-in to decisions, which yields greater commitment to action, which in turn leads to better results.

The Virtual Meetings Framework

How do you create highly engaging and highly productive virtual meetings? We have developed the virtual meetings framework as a guide for helping meeting leaders prepare and execute great virtual meetings. The framework is adapted from *The Secrets to Masterful Meetings*,[1] which serves as a basis for a number of tools and techniques described in this book. Let's walk through the framework's components.

Figure 1.2: The Virtual Meetings Framework

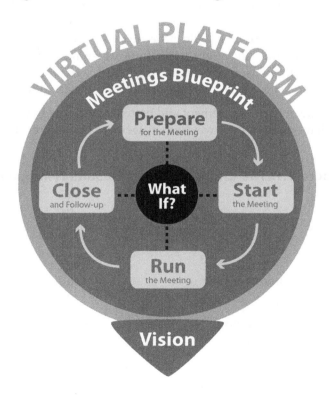

- At the base of the framework is the vision that describes the characteristics of a masterful virtual meeting. As you will see in future chapters, a masterful virtual meeting has sixteen important characteristics.

- From the vision flows the meetings blueprint, which includes strategies for preparing, starting, running, and closing masterful virtual meetings.

- A key component of the meetings blueprint is the "what if" element. What if someone is dominating the virtual meeting? What if someone verbally attacks another person? What if there is a major disagreement? The blueprint includes strategies for addressing these situations and more.

- Circling the meetings blueprint is the virtual platform that creates the environment for executing the meetings blueprint, which will help you achieve the vision of masterful virtual meetings.

What This Book Will Do for You

To be an effective leader of virtual meetings requires you to be proficient in the following three areas.

- You must know the features of the virtual meeting platform you are using.

- You should understand and be skilled in the principles of facilitating effective virtual meetings, including techniques for starting that get people excited about the meeting, asking questions, maintaining focus, building consensus, and addressing dysfunctional behaviors.

- You should have a toolbox of engagement strategies for keeping participants focused and productive in the virtual environment.

Through its twelve chapters, this book provides you a roadmap and strategies for achieving all three. Those familiar with *The Secrets of Facilitation*[2] and *The Secrets to Masterful Meetings* will recognize how the powerful facilitation techniques described in both have been adjusted and streamlined for the virtual environment. The book is divided into four parts, as described below.

Part I: The Virtual Revolution

Chapter
1

Why Virtual?

As you have read, this first chapter sets the stage for the shift to virtual, outlines the virtual meetings framework, describes the critical challenge of engaging in a virtual environment, and describes how this book meets the challenge. Key questions answered in this chapter include:

- Why are virtual meetings on the rise?
- Have virtual meeting skills improved proportionately with the rise in virtual meetings?
- What are the two fundamental issues with virtual meetings?
- Why is engagement so critical?
- What is the virtual meetings framework?
- What will this book do for you?

Chapter
2

Building a Virtual Meetings Vision

To provide strategies for success in a virtual environment, we must define what a masterful virtual meeting is. In this chapter we describe the sixteen characteristics of a masterful virtual meeting and the roles of meeting leaders and participants in creating meetings that deliver those characteristics. Key questions covered include these:

- What makes a virtual meeting different?
- Why haven't virtual meetings worked well?
- What are the problems to eliminate?
- What are the characteristics of a masterful virtual meeting?
- What is the role of a virtual meeting leader?
- What is the role of a virtual meeting participant?
- How do you eliminate unnecessary virtual meetings?

Chapter
3

Choosing a Virtual Meetings Platform

At the time of this publication, there were over fifty virtual meetings platforms from which to choose. In this chapter, we provide a framework that cuts through the noise and clutter by grouping virtual meetings platforms into four tiers based on the critical features they support. We then provide you with a process for determining which tier matters to you, and then a method for selecting the most appropriate tool in that tier. This chapter answers questions such as the following:

- What are the features that differentiate various products?

- Which features maximize participants' level of engagement and productivity in a virtual meeting?

- What are the four product tiers, and in which tier do some of the most common platforms fall?

- If you are choosing a virtual platform, how do you narrow your choices to one tier?

- Once you determine the appropriate tier, how do you select the right product within a tier?

Part II: Executing Virtual Meetings

Chapter
4

Preparing

Far too many virtual meetings fail due to a lack of planning and preparation. This chapter provides you an approach for planning for a virtual meeting and includes a comprehensive list of the items to cover in your preparation. The chapter shows you how to use the "six Ps" framework to maximize your time and eliminate unnecessary virtual meetings. The chapter also includes six common agendas to help shorten your preparation time. The following key questions are answered in this chapter:

- What are the six Ps for planning and preparing for a masterful virtual meeting?

- How do you avoid having unnecessary virtual meetings?

- How do you use the meeting's purpose and product to help develop the agenda?

- What are key ground rules for virtual meetings?

- How do you estimate the time for each agenda item?

- How do you plan for the level of engagement needed in a virtual environment?

- How do you prepare the virtual meeting room in advance?

Chapter 5

Starting

How a virtual meeting starts often sets participants' expectations for everything that follows. Start well and you create the expectation that the meeting will be engaging, effective, and well worth the time. Start poorly, however, and you can lose the participants even before you get to the first agenda item. In this chapter you will find the key for getting people engaged and excited about participating right from the start. You will also learn the strategy for asking great starting questions. This chapter answers the following:

- What are the key elements for an effective start to a virtual meeting?
- How do you reduce the likelihood that your meeting will be derailed by technical issues?
- What are strategies for getting the virtual meeting started on time?
- What are four things you should do in your opening statement to get people engaged and excited right away?
- What is Level 3 energy and how do you use it?
- How do you ask questions in such a way as to almost always receive lots of responses—instead of dreaded silence?
- How do you get people to buy in to the agenda?

Chapter 6

Running the Virtual Meeting

Once you have gotten your virtual meeting started, you will run the meeting by executing the agenda. But with each agenda item, there are key techniques to execute, including giving a checkpoint to get people focused right from the beginning, delivering clear directions, and reacting quickly to detours. Questions covered include the following:

- What should you do at the beginning of every agenda item to get the group focused?
- How do you give directions that are accurate, clear, and concise?
- What information needs to be documented during the session and what information doesn't?
- What do you do when someone tries to start an off-topic discussion?
- In a virtual meeting, what are the classic questions to avoid that meeting leaders ask but no one can answer?

Chapter
7

Gathering Information

Nearly every agenda item in a virtual meeting requires some type of information gathering process, such as brainstorming, or more frequently, presentation followed by questions. Unfortunately, most meeting leaders do not plan the processes that they will use; as a result, they employ the same one or two information gathering processes over and over again. Not only does this make meetings monotonous, but it also reduces engagement and effectiveness. Some agenda items may be better handled through using engagement strategies such as the whip, or using virtual platform features such as polling and whiteboarding. When you use the right process to address the specific need, and when you vary the way the process is done, meetings become more focused, more productive, and much more interesting for the participants. This chapter answers the following questions:

- What are the common information gathering processes?

- When and how do you use each one?

- How should you explain them to the group, and what starting questions should you ask?

- What does the output look like for the common information gathering processes?

Chapter
8

Closing and Follow-up

Once all agenda items have been covered, it is time to close the meeting. But prior to closing, there are a number of items to be covered, and after closing, follow-up is often needed. This chapter provides the framework for closing the virtual meeting in a masterful way. Key questions answered in this chapter include:

- What are the key components of a masterful close?

- How do you ensure buy-in and commitment to the decisions made in the meeting?

- What do you do with participants' key topics or their personal objectives identified at the beginning of the session?

- What do you do with the items remaining on the issues list?

- What are some guidelines for assigning responsibility for the actions list?

- What feedback is needed from the team and the meeting's sponsor?

- What should meeting notes from the session look like?

Part III: What If?

<table>
<tr>
<td>

Chapter

9

</td>
<td>

What If There Is Dysfunction?

Dysfunctional behavior can hinder the efficiency and effectiveness of a virtual meeting. There are many different types of dysfunctional behavior that can occur in a virtual meeting, ranging from dropping out and not participating to verbally attacking someone and leaving the virtual meeting room in disgust. This chapter focuses on strategies to consciously prevent, early detect, and cleanly resolve dysfunctional behavior.

The questions answered by this chapter include:

- What is the definition of dysfunctional behavior?
- What can you do *even before the meeting starts* to consciously prevent dysfunctional behavior from occurring?
- What early signs of dysfunction should you be on the lookout for?
- What is the general formula for resolving dysfunction?
- What are the common dysfunctions in a virtual meeting and what are specific strategies for preventing them, addressing them in the moment, and following up after the moment?
- What do you do if someone attacks the process?

</td>
</tr>
<tr>
<td>

Chapter

10

</td>
<td>

What If There Is Disagreement?

Most virtual meeting leaders don't know that there are only three reasons people disagree. They also lack the tools for diagnosing the level of disagreement and strategies for resolving each. Therefore, when a disagreement occurs, they are ill-equipped to address it. This chapter explains the reasons people disagree and provides five techniques for getting to yes when disagreements occur.

Key questions covered in this chapter include:

- What are the three reasons people disagree?
- How do you determine if a disagreement is Level 1, 2, or 3?
- What are strategies for addressing each of the three levels?
- What are the different criteria that teams use to define agreement?
- What is the informed majority process and when do you use it?
- What is five-finger consensus and why might it be a superior approach for gaining agreement on major decisions?

</td>
</tr>
</table>

Chapter
11

What If the Meeting Is a Special Case?

In most of this book we describe strategies for virtual meetings in which the meeting leader and most of the participants are in different locations. There are virtual meetings where this is not the case. The chapter covers three instances that represent special cases, and provides key strategies for the following situations:

- What if only a few people are remote?
- What if a large number of people are remote?
- What if you, the meeting leader, are the only person not in the room?

Part IV: A Sample Virtual Meeting

Chapter
12

Pulling It All Together

In this powerful final chapter, we demonstrate how to put the tools and techniques into use through the preparation, start, execution, and close of a two-hour virtual meeting. The chapter provides a comprehensive example of using the checklists for preparing for the meeting, getting the meeting started, running through the agenda items, and closing the meeting. You will see the following demonstrated:

Preparing

- The six Ps of preparation
- Developing the agenda
- Choosing the platform
- Determining the engagement methods
- Estimating the timing
- Developing a meeting notice
- Selecting ground rules
- Preparing the roll call list

Starting

- Minimizing technical issues
- Starting the meeting on time
- Delivering the opening
- Performing a roll call
- Engaging the participants
- Confirming the agenda
- Reviewing the ground rules
- Reviewing the parking boards
- Making introductions

Running the Meeting

- Using checkpoints to focus
- Giving directions using PeDeQs
- Asking starting questions that draw a vivid image
- Using round-robins
- Gaining consensus using informed majority
- Listing
- Brainstorming
- Whiteboarding
- Polling

Closing the Meeting

- Reviewing the items covered in the meeting
- Confirming decisions made
- Addressing outstanding issues

- Ensuring all actions have names and dates assigned
- Evaluating the meeting
- Thanking participants and ending the meeting

Through these twelve chapters we answer the questions posed by the virtual dilemma earlier in this chapter, "What will be different and how will I have to be different?"

Where appropriate throughout the book, we provide screenshots of the approaches we recommend so that you can see what is done. We use a variety of platforms in the screenshots to emphasize the point that the techniques that we present can be applied to almost any virtual platform you employ.

We end this first chapter with a case study that gives you a taste of the impact you will have when you use this book's virtual meeting strategies in your next meeting.

CASE STUDY
It's 4:00 a.m. Do You Know Where Your Facilitator Is?

(From author Michael Wilkinson)

When the client asked me to come back to the UK to facilitate a strategy update meeting, I knew it would be a problem. I had flown there a year ago to train a group of their facilitators to serve as breakout team leaders for a series of strategy sessions I facilitated, which, at one point, included their sixty top leaders. They had progressed well with the plan through the year, and the update was needed to review results and reset the strategic plan for the following year.

The one-day update would require a day of preparation. But because I was US-based, the trip to the UK would require a day of travel as well as another day to return. So my client would be paying a four-day fee to receive a one-day update. I wasn't sure the expense would justify the trip, so I recommended an alternative.

My suggestion was to hold two half-day virtual sessions. The sessions would go from 1 to 5 p.m. (their time) the first day and 9 a.m. to 1 p.m. on the second day. It took me a while to realize that the second session would be starting at 4 a.m. my time—and I had been the one to suggest it! Unfortunately, the client approved my suggestion before I came to my senses.

Figure 1.3: Case Study in Session

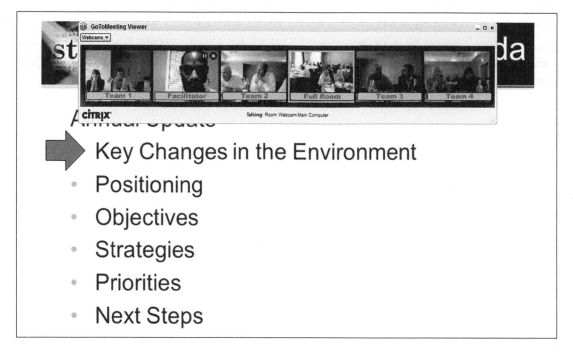

I started the meeting with the traditional "thank–excite–empower–involve" (see Chapter 5) and got the teams interacting right away using a "listing" exercise (see Chapter 7). I used frequent round-robins (see Chapter 7) to keep everyone engaged. We also had several breakout groups that I guided and commented on along the way.

At the end of the second day, the participants were asked to indicate what they liked about the session. Their responses were as follows; the number after an item indicates how many people made a similar comment.

- Pace (9)
- Structure (3)
- Participation (3)
- Preparation (2)
- Breakout facilitators (2)
- Primary facilitator not being here (we were more well-behaved) (2)
- Concentration levels

- Efficiency
- Engagement
- Enthusiasm for the session
- Great review process
- How we independently scored the priorities (shared view)
- Opportunity to rethink
- Web facilitation worked really well

There were three improvement suggestions: Have a bigger screen, distribute handout packages because the screen was so small, and have one of the facilitators in the room responsible for leading the review of flip chart information.

The closing comments from the head of the group were priceless: "When I learned that we were going to be doing this session with the facilitator virtual, I was very skeptical and did not think it could work. But I was pleasantly surprised. It was like you were in the room."

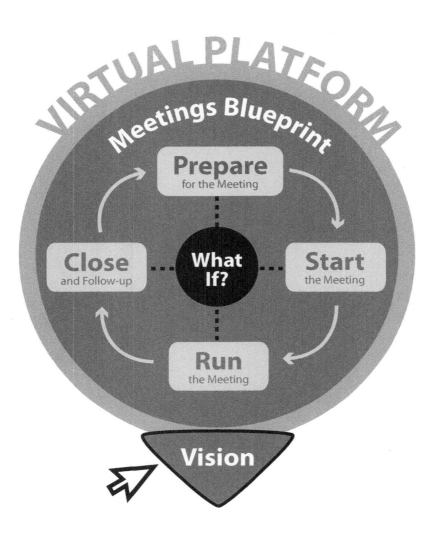

Building a Virtual Meeting Vision 2

The Virtual Dilemma

You are ready to schedule the first in a series of virtual sessions based on the cross-functional task force you have been asked to lead by the vice president of human capital. Although you have enjoyed success leading other task forces, these were all composed of participants at headquarters. With the majority of the members of this new task force located remotely in five different offices, you know this will be different.

As you prepare to schedule that first virtual meeting, you realize there are several things that you must consider. Among those are the following:

- Once you select a virtual meeting platform, how will you get the skills you need to lead these virtual sessions?

- What training will the participants need and how will you arrange it with them? How will you ensure the participants follow through with it? What will you do in the sessions to get the participants up to speed so that the task force can make the most of the virtual meeting platform's tools?

- What are the key differences between virtual and face-to-face meeting leadership that you will need to consider?

- Will you need different or special rules of engagement for the virtual meetings?

- How will you juggle both the meeting and the inevitable technical challenges that will occur using technology?

- What alternatives might you have to the typical engagement activities that you have used in face-to-face meetings to ensure the participants get involved and buy in to the task force's objectives?

You realize the importance of this task force to the VP of human capital, and the impact the results can have on your organization. You want to make sure this task force is a success. In addition, you would like to demonstrate how virtual meetings can be a powerful tool for reducing the expenses associated with the organization's face-to-face meetings, which include flying participants in for half-day sessions. This is your opportunity to validate a belief in the efficiency of virtual meetings and establish a precedent for how they can help the bottom line. To be successful, you have to answer two key questions.

***What does success look like with virtual meetings
and how do I achieve it?***

To create a vision of a successful virtual meeting, we start by identifying the common problems with virtual meetings and why they haven't worked well in the past.

The Problems with Virtual Meetings

Why are so many virtual meetings unengaging, uninspiring, unproductive, and ineffective? Participants in hundreds of our training sessions over the past two decades have repeatedly identified the following problems with face-to-face meetings. Virtual meetings are hampered by many of these same issues as listed below.[3]

Common problems shared by virtual and face-to-face meetings	• **Insufficient planning** surrounding the purpose, agenda, participants, timing, and information needed
	• **Lack of commitment** by participants to prepare for the meeting, arrive on time, stay until completion, and give full attention to the meeting topics
	• **Lack of interest and engagement** generated during the meeting that results in low energy and low participation
	• **Lack of control** by the meeting leader to keep the meeting on track and within time limits while maintaining an appropriate level of detail with balanced, respectful participation
	• **A sense of futility** by participants, believing that their efforts won't have an effect, or **a fear of retribution** if they speak up, causing them not to participate fully with open and honest dialogue
	• **Lack of respect** by meeting participants for each other as evidenced by such behaviors as interrupting one another, talking over one another, verbal attacks, and side conversations (such as in the platform's private chat feature)
	• **Inadequate decision-making processes**, leading to lack of consensus, decisions not being reached, conflict, or conflict-avoidance behaviors
	• **Insufficient follow-up** by not documenting decisions and assigning actions, or not following-up to ensure that assigned actions are completed.

In this book you will find strategies for addressing these common problems. Virtual meetings, however, have their own set of unique challenges. In the table that follows we identify ten problems unique to virtual meetings and also preview some of the techniques you will find in later chapters for addressing them.

Problems unique to virtual meetings

- **Lack of awareness that virtual meetings should be run differently,** and as a result, the meeting leader plans and executes the virtual meeting the same as a face-to-face meeting. This is a common problem and avoids addressing the key challenges of virtual meetings.

- **Inadequate planning for the technological glitches associated with virtual meeting platforms** often derails virtual meetings right from the start. While planning can't prevent all issues, having a plan can eliminate some issues and minimize the impact of others. In later chapters we will discuss the importance of instructing people to test the use of the technology before the meeting, as well as other strategies for minimizing the impact of glitches.

- **The meeting leader tries to run the meeting while also addressing people's technical difficulties**, which causes the leader to do a poor job of both. With virtual meetings of more than a few people, we recommend having a moderator whose job it is to assist participants with questions about the technology and to help with the meeting's flow. This frees the leader to focus on starting, executing, and closing the meeting.

- **Assuming participants are equally well-versed in using the virtual meeting platform** can result in less skilled participants dropping out or reducing their involvement. Advance training and orientation can minimize these issues.

- **Not preparing in advance for when and how participants will use various features of the tool** results in lost opportunities to increase productivity, effectiveness, and engagement. During your preparation, you can augment your agenda design with details about how you will use the virtual meeting tool.

- **The increased likelihood that participants will multi-task** in virtual meetings means that the meeting leader must adjust by both increasing the frequency of engagement as well as varying the types of activities. When the meeting does not include video that allows everyone to see one another, participants can frequently disengage to work on other activities unless specific steps are taken to maintain their interest. Engagement in any meeting is important; but in virtual meetings, since the meeting leader is unable to read body language, engagement is even more critical. The frequent use of polls, whiteboarding, round-robins, and other engagement strategies can make a significant difference. You will see that we recommend some type of engagement every ten to twenty minutes in a virtual meeting.

Problems unique to virtual meetings
(continued)

- **The difficulty in "reading the room" and detecting dysfunctional behavior** before it becomes a problem can be significant. While the use of video technology can provide some visual cues, missing the early signs of dysfunction can be disastrous. The use of frequent engagement strategies, as well as having a moderator to monitor the question-and-answer panels and view participants' chatting, can help detect dysfunction. Careful preparation in the placement of webcams helps, as well, as does assigning someone to be the "eyes and ears" of the meeting leader in cases where multiple participants are in the same room.

- **The inability to pick up on early signs of disagreement** poses a challenge to the leader who has not adjusted to the virtual environment by using frequent consensus checks, polling, whiteboards, the "raising of hands," and other features that may be a part of the virtual meeting platform.

- **The lifeless virtual meeting leader** is a frequent issue because many meeting leaders do not recognize the importance of compensating for the lack of face-to-face energy. We find it helpful to run virtual meetings at what we call **Energy Level 3** (versus Energy Level 1, which is a normal speaking voice). We also stand occasionally when we are leading a virtual meeting. Both of these techniques can project the extra energy that can make a big difference in keeping the virtual meeting participants awake and engaged.

- **Poor timing of a virtual meeting across multiple time zones** can lead to overall poor performance by many participants. Timing can be a scheduling issue as well as an issue of duration. With multiple time zones common, the time of day for all participants may not be ideal. And while we frequently lead multi-day meetings for our clients, we find that virtual meetings should be limited to two hours or less unless offering a substantial break of thirty minutes or more.

While these lists may appear daunting, the good news is that there are tools and techniques to address them. In Part II of this book, we will share with you our best practices for conducting what we call masterful virtual meetings.

The Characteristics of a Masterful Virtual Meeting

Masterful virtual meeting is the term we use to refer to a vision of what we believe every virtual meeting should be. In summary, a masterful virtual meeting can be described as follows:

> A masterful virtual meeting is a well-prepared, well-executed, and results-oriented meeting in which one or more participants are not in the same room; the meeting has a timely start, a decisive close, and a clear follow-up plan.

Masterful virtual meetings have sixteen specific characteristics, as shown in Figure 2.1, which overcome the problems described in prior pages.

Figure 2.1: Characteristics of Masterful Virtual Meetings

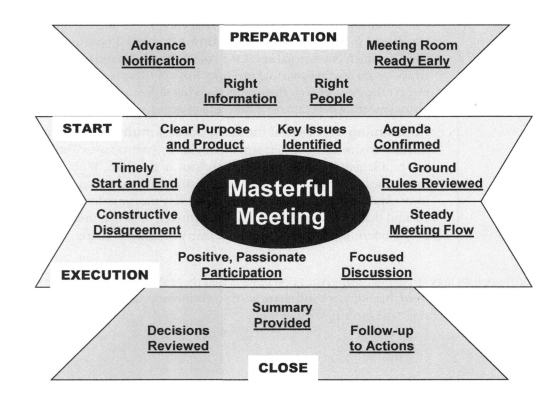

Preparation

1. **Advance notification**
   Participants know the purpose, desired products, proposed agenda, and other important information about the meeting in advance.

2. **Virtual meeting room ready early**
   The meeting leader arrives in the virtual meeting room early enough so that the room is set up and running at least ten minutes before the virtual meeting begins.

3. **Right people—prepared and present**
   The right people are included in the virtual meeting. They arrive prepared and skilled in the use of the virtual meeting platform. They arrive on time and stay for the duration. Where necessary, a moderator is available to assist the meeting leader with participant questions and any technical issues that arise.

4. **Right information**
   All necessary information is available at the virtual meeting.

Start

5. **Timely start and end**
   The virtual meeting starts and ends on time.

6. **Clear purpose and products**
   At the start of the virtual meeting, the meeting leader reviews the meeting's purpose and desired products.

7. **Key topics identified**
   Either during the virtual meeting or in advance, all participants have a chance to identify key topics that need to be discussed to achieve the purpose and products.

8. **Agenda confirmed**
   The virtual meeting leader confirms the agenda and establishes time limits for each item. The leader may choose to adjust the agenda to ensure all key issues are discussed.

9. **Ground rules reviewed**
   The virtual meeting leader reminds the participants of ground rules. Participants honor the ground rules throughout the meeting.

Execution

10. Steady meeting flow
As the virtual meeting flows from one agenda item to the next, the meeting leader reminds the participants of the purpose for each agenda item, how the agenda item fits into the overall meeting objective, and what the group is being asked to accomplish with the agenda item.

11. Focused discussion
The discussion remains focused on the topic at hand. A topic is allowed to exceed its allotted time only with the express agreement of a majority and with full knowledge of the effect on the remaining agenda items.

12. Positive, passionate participation
All virtual meeting participants are actively engaged throughout the meeting. They feel it is safe to speak openly and honestly. People talk and listen with respect. There is energized discussion and debate. No one is allowed to dominate the discussion.

13. Constructive conflict
Disagreement is encouraged and conflict is handled by participants asking questions, identifying strengths, defining concerns, and seeking new alternatives that maximize strengths and reduce concerns.

Close and Follow-up

14. Decisions and actions reviewed
During the virtual meeting, issues that arise that are inappropriate for discussion are deferred to an issues list; decisions made and actions to be taken are documented. Prior to ending the virtual meeting, all issues, decisions, and actions are reviewed, and appropriate action designated.

15. Summary provided
Following the virtual meeting, a meeting summary is distributed to all participants identifying issues, decisions, actions, and relevant analysis.

16. Follow up on actions
A follow-up process is put in place to ensure all assigned actions are performed.

What Do Masterful Virtual Meeting Leaders Do?

Given the characteristics of masterful virtual meetings, it is the meeting leaders who are ultimately responsible for ensuring their virtual meetings are masterful. While you will find details on planning, starting, running, and closing virtual meetings in Part II, the list that follows summarizes the role of virtual meeting leaders.

Planning and Preparing

1. Determine the virtual meeting type, purpose, and products.

2. Select participants and arrange for a trained moderator for virtual meetings as appropriate. (We find when the meeting has more than seven to ten participants a moderator is essential for a successful virtual meeting.)

3. Identify probable issues that need to be addressed.

4. Develop the proposed agenda.

5. Select the processes that will be used to execute the agenda, and define the engagement strategies appropriate for the virtual meeting.

6. Hold discussions as needed before the meeting.

7. Select the virtual meeting platform and handle any other logistics.

8. Prepare and distribute the virtual meeting notice.

Starting Meetings

9. Set up the virtual meeting room, including any parking boards that will be used.

10. Greet people when they arrive in the virtual meeting room.

11. Provide a two-minute warning before the virtual meeting begins.

12. Start the virtual meeting by stating its purpose and products.

13. Ask participants to identify key topics to be discussed.

14. Review the proposed agenda; modify as needed to address the key topics; establish time limits for each item.

15. Remind the participants of the ground rules and parking boards.

16. Make introductions if needed.

Running, Closing, and Following Up

17. Review prior action items to ensure follow-up.

18. For each agenda item: (FIRST CLASS)

    - **F**ocus the participants by providing an explanation of how the item furthers the meeting's purpose.
    - **I**nstruct by providing clear and concise directions on how the agenda item will be executed.
    - **R**ecord the appropriate information gathered during the virtual meeting, or ensure the information is recorded.
    - **S**tep the participants through the agenda item, using the appropriate information gathering process.
    - **T**rack time to ensure that the participants are using time appropriately.
    - **C**ontrol and resolve any dysfunctional behavior quickly and effectively.
    - **L**isten for off-topic discussions and redirect to a parking board to keep the meeting focused.
    - **A**ddress disagreements or conflicts that emerge.
    - **S**eek all opinions, and invite people to speak.
    - **S**ummarize the results.

19. Close the meeting.

    - Review the items covered in the virtual meeting.
    - Confirm the decisions made.
    - Address outstanding issues.
    - Ensure that all actions have names and dates assigned.

20. Perform meeting follow-ups.

    - Document and distribute meeting notes.
    - Follow up to hold people accountable for their assigned actions.

What Is the Participants' Role in Masterful Virtual Meetings?

Just as meeting leaders have a role in creating masterful virtual meetings, so do the meeting's participants. The table that follows, Figure 2.2, summarizes the Dos and Don'ts of participating in masterful virtual meetings.

Figure 2.2: Role of Participants in a Masterful Virtual Meeting

Do	Don't
Show up on time, prepared to meet, having reviewed all materials provided in advance, and having an understanding of how to use the virtual meeting platform.	Show up late, unprepared, or unable to use the virtual meeting platform.
Show respect to all present.	Speak while others have the floor, speak in a condescending tone, verbally attack or interrupt others by speaking over them while they are talking, or having side chats with other participants unless this is acceptable to the group.
Speak positive points first.	Start with negative comments.
Speak up when you disagree or don't understand.	Remain silent despite disagreement.
Give your name each time you speak, if video is not available, until participants readily can associate voices and names.	Speak without giving your name.
Share the air, giving others the opportunity to speak.	Dominate the discussion.
Share intent and all relevant information.	Hide intent, conceal information, or allow relevant issues to go unspoken.
Seek to understand by asking questions.	Disengage when you are not speaking or only focus on the point you want to make without listening to others.
Seek win–win solutions that satisfy all needs.	Insist your point of view is right and all others are wrong.
Stay focused on the topic and alert at all times.	Wander off topic or get engaged with other work (e.g., cell phone, PDA, IM, e-mail).
Stay present for the entire meeting.	Leave before the completion or scheduled completion of the meeting.

What Is the Role of Training in Realizing the Vision?

Agreeing on a vision of what a masterful virtual meeting looks like is not enough to bring that vision into reality. Masterful virtual meetings don't occur on their own. They require more planning, more preparation, and more focused execution than their face-to-face counterparts.

Unfortunately, as virtual meetings become more common, we are finding that most people try to transfer their generally poor face-to-face meeting habits into the much more challenging virtual world. Why do we rate these habits as "generally poor"? Consider the following points.

- How many leaders of face-to-face meetings have a clearly defined purpose and product before calling a meeting?

- How many of these leaders welcome dissenting points of view, and know how to skillfully use disagreement to create better solutions?

- How many understand why various dysfunctions occur in meetings and how to preempt them?

- How many use a variety of strategies to keep people focused and engaged?

The lack of these skills in the face-to-face world generally leads to a high percentage of ineffective, inefficient, and unengaging meetings. And, unfortunately, we are seeing this same result multiplied in the virtual world, where a lack of engagement can be downright deadly for a virtual meeting.

While there are a number of virtual meeting training programs available, most are not designed to address these skill deficiencies. Many training programs for the virtual world instead focus most of their time teaching participants how to use the tool. Skills for running a masterful virtual meeting tend to be an afterthought and relegated to a very small percentage of the training time, as shown in Figure 2.3.

Figure 2.3: The Focus of Many Virtual Meeting Training Courses

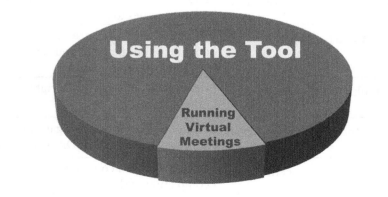

How important is it that training sessions focus on how to run masterful virtual meetings? Eric Bensley, senior product marketing manager for GoToMeeting, recommends that, when it comes to virtual meetings training, at least 90 percent of the time should be spent on training to run effective virtual meetings versus training on using the virtual tool. As he put it, "If you have to spend money for training on the tool, you are probably buying the wrong tool."

A Recommended Approach to Virtual Meeting Training

Figure 2.4 shows a more integrated approach to virtual meeting training, where the focus of the training is on how to run a masterful virtual meeting. With this approach, tool mastery is integrated within the training so that you are learning how to use the tool while you are learning how to skillfully plan, prepare, and execute virtual meetings.

Figure 2.4: A Recommended Focus for Virtual Meeting Training

We believe that there are several key skills that an integrated training approach should provide. We've listed ten in particular, here.

- What are the steps for planning for a virtual meeting?
- Based on my plan, how do I prepare the virtual tool in advance?
- How do I start the meeting in a way that gets people immediately engaged?
- As we move through the agenda, how do I keep people focused?
- What are different ways to engage participants and how do I use the virtual tool for each one?
- How do I use questions to effectively get participants to own the results?
- What do I do before the meeting to prevent dysfunctional behavior?

- What are the common dysfunctions that occur in a virtual meeting and what should I do if they occur?

- What are the key reasons people disagree and what strategies can I use for addressing each?

- How do I masterfully close the meeting?

Of course, the integrated approach is what we advocate and the approach we employ. The chapters included in Parts II and III of this book will give you strategies covering each of the items listed above. In addition, you can find more information on our training approach to virtual meetings in the About Leadership Strategies section of this book.

When Should a Meeting NOT Be Virtual?

Virtual meetings can be an effective way to have a needed interaction, but they are not always appropriate. While there is no right or wrong answer concerning which meetings should be conducted face to face and which meetings should be conducted virtually, Figure 2.5 is an approach for evaluating this dilemma.

Figure 2.5: When Should a Meeting NOT Be Virtual?

		Loss of Effectiveness If Virtual		
		Low	Medium	High
Additional Cost of Meeting Face to Face	High	Virtual	Virtual	?
	Med	Virtual	?	Face-to-Face
	Low	?	Face-to-Face	Face-to-Face

The key conclusions summarized in this table include:

- In most instances, if you compare the cost of meeting face to face with the cost of meeting virtually, the face-to-face costs are higher. This is largely due to the costs related to the time getting to the meeting, expenses associated with traveling to the meeting, additional facility costs if needed, etc., as shown in Figure 2.6.

Figure 2.6: Travel Costs, Face-to-Face versus Virtual

Meeting of seven people, two local and five remote for a two-day virtual meeting

Face-to-Face Meeting	Expense	Virtual Meeting
$2,000	Airline travel (average airline ticket of $400/ remote participant)	$0
$250	Local transportation ($50/remote participant to/from airport to hotel and return)	$0
$400	Meals ($40/remote person/day for 2 days)	$0
$250	Mileage and parking ($50/remote person)	$0
$0	Facilities Cost (room charges if necessary)	$0
$2,900	Total Expenses	**$0**

Note: See the "Virtual Resource for You" section at the end of this chapter for a meeting cost calculator you can use to estimate the cost of your meetings.

- This would tend to suggest that any time the cost of meeting face to face is higher, then the economically prudent thing to do is to meet virtually.

- In many cases, however, there is some loss of effectiveness when meeting virtually. The loss might be due to people not staying focused on the task, people not being able to read body language, etc. By mastering the engagement strategies included in this book you will be able to better address these challenges. If you are using a virtual meeting platform, you can use the Levels of Effectiveness and Productivity Chart discussed in the next chapter as a guide for determining how much engagement and productivity you lose, theoretically, with the platform chosen.

- In general, when the additional cost of meeting face to face is low or when the loss of effectiveness of meeting virtually is high, a face-to-face meeting should be used.

- In most cases, when the cost of meeting face to face is high or when the loss of effectiveness of meeting virtually is low, virtual meetings should be used.

- When both the additional cost of meeting face to face and the loss of effectiveness of meeting virtually are low, medium, or high, it appears that an organization can decide based on its bias. For organizations with a bias toward face-to-face interaction, they would likely choose in-person meetings; for those with a bias toward virtual, they would likely choose virtual ones.

Note that only recently has technology advanced to the point where a discussion about the option of virtual meetings exists for nearly every meeting. We believe the earlier lack of virtual tools meant that the loss of effectiveness with virtual meetings was so high that the entire "low" column essentially did not exist. There are also organizations that remain so uncomfortable with virtual meetings that all nine cells in this table would essentially be labeled "face-to-face."

With a combination of increased pressure to reduce costs, the continued advancement of technology, and a generation of businesspeople accustomed to being connected virtually, the future growth of virtual meetings appears to be inevitable.

Special Topic: Meeting Types

To hold a masterful virtual meeting, it is important to recognize that there are three basic meeting types: status meetings, working meetings, and strategy meetings. The meeting type is determined by whether the primary focus of the participants will be reviewing, creating, or direction setting, as shown in Figure 2.7.

Figure 2.7: Meeting Types

	Status Meeting	Working Meeting	Strategy Meeting
Meeting Focus	Review	Creation	Direction setting
Meeting Flow	Primarily one-way	Primarily two-way	Primarily two-way
Typical Products	Information update, idea generation, feedback	Decision, issue resolution, action plan	Strategic direction, broad plan, priorities
Group Size	Unlimited	3–16	3–16
Typical Length	30–90 minutes	1–3 hours	1–4 days
Typical Frequency	Weekly, monthly	As needed	Quarterly

While strategy meetings are typically one to four days, it is unusual to have a virtual meeting for this purpose (though in our line of work, we have done it more than a few times). Therefore, in our discussion below, we will focus on the differences between status and working meetings in the virtual environment. For the sake of the discussion, you can think of strategy meetings as being extended working meetings.

The Differences

- While virtual status meetings are designed to review progress or gain feedback, virtual working meetings are designed to create a decision, action plan, or some other product; and strategy meetings are designed to set a direction.

- Virtual status meetings are primarily one-way communication and therefore can have three, thirty, or three hundred people. The number of meeting participants may affect your choice of virtual meeting platform, though.

- Virtual working meetings require two-way communication and should have a much smaller number of participants. The number of participants is an important factor in the selection of an appropriate virtual meeting platform.

- And while virtual status meetings tend to be relatively short since they are review meetings, virtual working meetings tend to be longer because creation typically takes more time.

A Common Problem with Virtual Status Meetings

Unfortunately, one of the most common problems with status meetings is that they become working meetings! That is, in the middle of the virtual status meeting, the meeting leader discovers a problem and takes time during the virtual status meeting to develop solutions.

Why is it a problem for a virtual status meeting to include problem solving? Let's create a hypothetical but fairly common example. Imagine a virtual meeting with the meeting leader and ten others assembled for a virtual status meeting.

Sample Status Meeting Problem

- Each of the ten members has been allotted five minutes to provide a status update as part of this one-hour virtual meeting, with ten minutes of cushion available as needed. What happens?

- By the fourth person, the ten-minute cushion has already been eaten up by two problem-solving detours.

- During each of the problem-solving detours, those not involved in the discussion put themselves on hold, and start using e-mail or texting while waiting for the status meeting to continue.

- By the seventh person, there are only ten minutes left to split among the last four, so their reviews are rushed.

- The tenth person has a pressing issue that turns out to be more important than any of the others that took up the additional time.

Solving the Virtual Status Meeting Problem

- You can prevent virtual status meetings from becoming virtual working meetings by using half the time to update statuses and identify issues, and the other half to address the most critical issues identified.

- For a virtual status meeting, consider posting the statuses and issues prior to the meeting so all participants can review items in advance.

- When an important problem is identified during the status updates, the virtual meeting leader should add the issue to the list of items to be addressed when the virtual status meeting is over.

- Once the statuses of all items are complete, the virtual meeting leader should review the outstanding issues, allocate appropriate time among them, and continue to meet with key participants.

- For all others, the virtual status meeting is over!

A Common Problem with Virtual Working Meetings

While virtual working meetings are specifically designed to solve problems and virtual strategy meetings to set direction, both virtual meeting types have the tendency to become *another* virtual working meeting. Let's use an example of a virtual working meeting convened to address problems with the hiring process.

Sample the Virtual Working Meeting Problem

- The discussion starts with identifying several problems, including the cost and level of service from the organization's health insurance provider.

- One person suggests that we might have a different provider if there were more diversity within HR and on the panel that does provider selection.

- What ensues is a twenty-minute debate over whether HR and the panel need greater diversity.

While a case could be made that the team is attempting to get at the root cause of the costs and level of service from the health insurance provider, they may have lost sight of their core issue: problems with the hiring process and how to address them. They have instead detoured to a new topic: diversity in HR. As you will see in Part III, to address the topic jumper and prevent detours, the meeting leader can respond as follows.

Solving the Virtual Working Meeting Problem

- "That may be a very valid point about diversity and something to investigate later. Can we put that on our list of potential issues to discuss, and get back to identifying other problems that directly affect our hiring process?"

An understanding of the difference between virtual status meetings, virtual working meetings, and virtual strategy meetings will guide your selection of the appropriate purpose, products, and participants during preparation, which will be covered in Part II.

Eliminating Meetings

We conclude this chapter on building a vision for masterful virtual meetings by focusing on ways to eliminate the unnecessary ones. Meetings, whether face-to-face or virtual, take time and tie up resources. Therefore, if a quality result can be achieved without holding a meeting, this is often preferred.

Eliminating Virtual Status Meetings

- If the virtual meeting is truly "information only," consider distributing a memo or using voicemail.
- If little action has taken place between virtual status meetings, consider making these meetings less frequent.

Eliminating Virtual Working Meetings and Virtual Strategy Meetings

- Make analysis assignments and perform the analysis outside of a meeting.
- Document a preliminary decision in written form and circulate it for comment. Consider posting the analysis so it is available in the virtual meeting room.

Questions to Ask before Calling a Virtual Meeting

If someone asks you to attend a virtual meeting, or if you are thinking about holding a virtual meeting yourself, ask the following questions.

- What is the purpose of calling the meeting?
- Is it possible to achieve the purpose without a meeting?
- Is the purpose worth the time and resources that the virtual meeting will consume?

Summary: The Strategies for Building a Virtual Meeting Vision

In summary, to increase the effectiveness of virtual meetings in your organization, we recommend that you and your team embrace the following strategies from this chapter on building a virtual meetings vision:

Strategy 1.　　Ensure that your team understands the common problems with virtual and face-to-face meetings and the unique problems with virtual meetings.

Strategy 2.　　Establish a vision of a masterful virtual meeting that addresses both the common and the unique problems.

Strategy 3.　　Define and communicate the role of virtual meeting leaders and the role of virtual meeting participants.

Strategy 4.　　Educate meeting leaders and participants on the different meeting types, their differences, and when each is appropriate.

Strategy 5.　　Equip meeting leaders and participants with the questions to ask for determining if a meeting is really necessary and for eliminating unnecessary ones.

Strategy 6.　　Assess which meetings can be conducted virtually versus face to face and document the cost savings associated with conducting virtual meetings.

Virtual Resource for You

The following resource is available on the Virtual Meetings Website to aid you in implementing the strategies in this chapter.

Want to estimate the cost of a meeting?
Our meeting cost calculator may be able to help.
www.virtualmeetingsbook.com/calculator

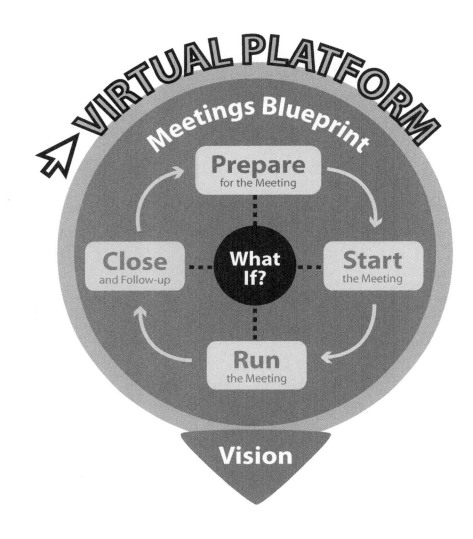

Choosing a Virtual Meeting Platform 3

- The Virtual Dilemma
- Levels of Engagement and Productivity
- Overview of Virtual Meeting Platforms
- Virtual Meeting Platforms by Product Tier
- Comparison of Selected Virtual Meeting Platforms
- Feature Glossary
- Selecting a Virtual Meetings Platform
- Summary: The Strategies for Choosing a Virtual Platform
- Virtual Resource for You

The Virtual Dilemma

As you begin planning for the cross-functional task force on improving the performance review process, you recognize that part of the assignment includes choosing a tool for planning and conducting virtual meetings. In investigating the numerous virtual meeting platforms available, you realize the choices are much more varied than you expected. What you thought would be the typical Windows-versus-Macintosh operating system dilemma has become significantly more complicated. You realize that part of your success with the assignment will be your platform decision.

Some of the questions you have are as follows:

- What criteria should you use to evaluate the vendor platforms for conducting virtual meetings?

- Since there are some no-cost options, should you save the company money by selecting one of these?

- What are the key features and functions that you will need to conduct masterful virtual meetings?

Your choice will be important to the vice president of human capital, because the results of your meeting will affect the organization. The virtual meeting platform you pick will likely be rolled out for use by a much broader audience after your task force is successful. You want to make sure this virtual meeting platform decision is the right one.

How should you go about determining which platform is right for you?

At the time of this publication, there were over fifty virtual meeting platforms from which to choose. In this chapter, we provide a framework that cuts through the clutter by grouping virtual meetings platforms into tiers based on the critical features they support. We then provide you with a process for determining which tier to focus on, and then a method for selecting the most appropriate tool in that tier. Let's start by understanding how the virtual meeting platform can affect participants' engagement and productivity.

Levels of Engagement and Productivity

The virtual meeting platform you use can supercharge the group's level of engagement. Of course the skills of the meeting leader, the motivation of the participants, and other factors can impact both engagement and productivity. But in general, the capability of the virtual platform provides an engagement foundation as well. If we set 10 as a group's average level of engagement and productivity (LEP) when you are holding a face-to-face meeting, and 1 as the average LEP for a conference call, Figure 3.1 gives our estimate of how the virtual meeting platform capability generally affects the LEP of a business meeting.

Figure 3.1: Levels of Engagement and Productivity

Virtual Meeting Platform Feature	LEP	Comment
Audio only (conference call)	1	People can hear one another.
Audio and desktop sharing	3	People can hear one another and see the same information.
Audio and video	4	People can hear one another and see one another.
Audio, video, and desktop sharing	6	People can hear one another, see one another, and view the same information.
Audio, video, desktop sharing, and whiteboard	7	People can hear one another, see one another, view the same information, and provide written input at the same time.
Audio, video, desktop sharing, whiteboard, and breakout groups	8	People can hear one another, see one another, view the same information, provide written input at the same time, and work in sub-teams.
Face-to-face meeting	10	People can hear one another, see one another, view the same information, provide written input at the same time, work in sub-teams, fully observe non-verbal communication, and physically interact (e.g., shake hands).

There are three points in particular worth highlighting from this chart.

- We consider using audio and desktop sharing capability (rating 3) as three times more engaging and productive as using audio alone (rating 1). We find that using a desktop sharing platform provides a center of focus for the discussion and typically yields quicker and more collaborative results.

- Adding a whiteboard and video (rating 8) is more than twice as productive as audio and desktop sharing (rating 3). When people can see one another and provide written input simultaneously, both engagement and productivity jump.

- Given the level of engagement and productivity provided by various combinations of features, we use this information to help define product tiers, as you will see in the next section.

Overview of Virtual Meeting Platforms

How do you go about choosing a virtual meeting platform? For many virtual meeting leaders, the choice of a virtual platform is not a choice at all. Your organization may have already selected a platform. If you are faced with choosing a virtual meeting platform, however, you will find that you have over fifty options that are as varied as the breadth of features they provide.

The virtual meeting platform landscape is changing rapidly. Newcomers are piling up in the field and old leaders are becoming "also rans," and some are even being sunsetted in favor of newer products. But at the time of this writing, we divide virtual meeting platforms into four product tiers as shown in Figure 3.2.

Figure 3.2: Product Tier Table

1	Full Features*	Includes basic features such as video and desktop sharing, as well as advanced features such as annotation, breakouts, polling, and whiteboards.
2	Basic Features	Includes basic features such as video and desktop sharing, but typically does not include one or more of the following: annotation, breakouts, polling, and whiteboards.
3	Limited Features	Excludes one or more basic features such as video or desktop sharing, or supports fewer than fifteen users.
4	Special Purpose	Provides features for a special purpose or a special audience.

A glossary containing feature definitions appears later in this chapter.

Virtual Meeting Platforms by Product Tier

Figure 3.3 categorizes a number of platforms available at the time of this writing. For information about these platforms and an updated version of this table with additional virtual platforms, go to **www.virtualmeetingsbook.com/vendors.**

Figure 3.3: Virtual Meeting Platforms by Product Tier

	1 Full	2 Basic	3 Limited	4 Special
Adobe Connect	X			
Live Meeting	X			
Spreed	X			
WebEx	X			
ClickMeeting		X		
4Webcom		X		
GoToMeeting		X		
RHUB		X		
WizIQ		X		
Hangouts			X	
Join.Me			X	
Lync			X	
Skype			X	
Blackboard Collaborate				X
Power Noodle				X

Comparison of Selected Virtual Meeting Platforms

To provide you a view of how platforms are different, Figure 3.4 summarizes the features of six of the more popular virtual meeting platforms in use at the time of this writing, two from each of the top three product tiers. To get the most current information on the features of these virtual meeting platforms as well as others, see the "Virtual Resource for You" section at the end of this chapter.

Figure 3.4: Comparison of Selected Virtual Meeting Platforms

		Adobe	Cisco	Citrix	Implix	Google	LogMeIn
		Adobe Connect	WebEx	GoTo-Meeting	Click-Meeting	Hangouts	Join.Me
	Product Tier	**1**	**1**	**2**	**2**	**3**	**3**
Advanced	Annotation capability	Yes	Yes	No	No	No	No
	Breakout rooms	Yes	Yes	No	No	No	No
	Polling	Yes	Yes	No	Yes	No	No
	Whiteboard	Yes	Yes	No	No	No	No
Basic/Limited	Chat	Yes	Yes	Yes	Yes	Yes	Yes
	Desktop sharing	Yes	Yes	Yes	Yes	No	Yes
	Recording	Yes	Yes	Yes	Yes	No	No
	Transfer mouse control	Yes	Yes	Yes	Yes	No	No
	Transfer presenter	Yes	Yes	Yes	Yes	No	No
	Video/webcam	Yes	Yes	Yes	Yes	Yes	No
	VoIP	Yes	Yes	Yes	Yes	Yes	Yes
Other	Asynch. capability	No	No	No	Yes	No	No
	Moderator	Yes	Yes	Yes	Yes	No	No
	Maximum number of participants	100	100	25	1,000	10	250
Costs	Pay per use	Yes	Yes	No	No	No	No
	Costs	$$$	$$	$$	$	NC	NC

Feature Glossary

A description of each of the features listed in Figure 3.4 follows, in the order in which they appear in the table.

Advanced

- Annotation capability: Allows participants to type directly onto the content being shown in the virtual meeting.

- Breakout rooms: Allows the meeting leader to establish smaller subgroups of participants to meet and interact by voice, and includes a common whiteboard in separate "rooms" during the virtual meeting—much like the use of breakout groups in a face-to-face meeting.

- Polling: Allows the meeting leader to prepare survey questions to which participants respond during a virtual meeting.

- Whiteboard: Allows the meeting leader to provide a typing space for the presenter and other participants to record comments (the analogy of a whiteboard or flip chart in a face-to-face meeting).

Basic/Limited

- Chat: Allows participants to send messages to an individual or the entire group while the meeting is in progress.

- Desktop sharing: Allows meeting participants to view the leader's desktop (and in some platforms, sharing may be transferred to other participants as well as the meeting leader).

- Recording: Allows recording of the meeting for viewing after the completion of the virtual meeting.

- Transfer mouse control: Allows the meeting leader to transfer control of the mouse to a participant during the virtual meeting.

- Transfer presenter: Allows the meeting leader to transfer presentation control to other participants who can then share their desktop or perform other functions as the presenter.

- Video/webcam: Allows participants to see one another through the transmission of video using webcams during the virtual meeting.

- VoIP: Allows the use of Voice-over-IP for audio communication during the virtual meeting; this feature typically would cancel the need for using telephones for hearing the virtual meeting.

Other

- Asynchronous capability: Allows participants to access the meeting room and provide information anytime as opposed to during a scheduled meeting time.

- Upgrade to moderator: Allows the meeting leader to "promote" other participants by giving them moderation capability, allowing them to assist in running the virtual meeting.

Costs

- Pay per use: Indicates whether there is a "usage charge" for participants in addition to any license fee associated with the virtual meeting platform.

- Costs: Indicates monthly costs for twenty-five users with the features listed: NC/No cost, $/Under $25, $$/under $50, $$$/under $100, $$$$/$100 or more.

- Maximum number of participants: The maximum number of virtual meeting participants for any virtual meeting (based on the costs indicated).

Selecting a Virtual Meetings Platform

How do you go about selecting a virtual meetings platform? We recommend the following steps.

1. **Determine the why, the what, and the constraints.** Find out why the organization is moving to virtual and what is needed before tackling how to best meet the need. Be sure to identify any specific constraints.

The Why	Why is the organization moving to virtual meetings? What is the overall business objective that the organization is trying to accomplish and how will we measure the success of virtual meetings?
The What	What types of meetings will be conducted virtually? What will likely be the maximum number of participants?
The Constraints	What constraints (e.g., budget, timing) do we have that must be considered in selecting a virtual meetings platform?

2. **View a variety of platforms.** To gain an understanding and appreciation of the various features, view at least two or three platforms in each of the product tiers.

3. **Identify the most critical product features.** After viewing a variety of platforms, determine the critical three to seven features that best enable you to achieve your "what" and "why."

4. **Narrow your choices based on product tiers**. Once you have selected the critical product features, use the Product Tier Selection Matrix, Figure 3.5, as a guide in deciding the product tier or tiers from which to choose.

Figure 3.5: Product Tier Selection Matrix

	Product Tiers			
	1 Full	**2** Basic	**3** Limited	**4** Special
To maximize engagement, it is important to have annotation, breakout rooms, polling, or whiteboard.	√	Eliminate		
To increase productivity, it is important for everyone to see one another and to see the leader's desktop.	√	√	Eliminate	
More than twenty-five people need to attend the virtual meeting at the same time.	√	√	Eliminate Most	√
The virtual meeting platform must be free.	Eliminate		√	Eliminate

5. **Select the platform**. Once you have narrowed your tiers, review various platforms within the product tiers and select the one that best meets your needs, given your constraints.

Summary: The Strategies for Choosing a Virtual Platform

In summary, the strategies for choosing a virtual meeting platform for your organization include the following:

Strategy 7. Find out why the organization is moving to virtual and what is needed, being sure to identify specific budget constraints and other requirements.

Strategy 8. View a variety of platforms to gain an understanding of features.

Strategy 9. Determine your critical three to seven features needed.

Strategy 10. Narrow your choices to the product tier for your critical features.

Strategy 11. Select the virtual meeting platform that best meets your needs and constraints.

Virtual Resource for You

The following resource is available on the Virtual Meetings Website to aid you in implementing the strategies in this chapter.

If you are selecting a virtual meeting platform, you may find it helpful to have an updated version of Figure 3.3 showing video meeting platforms sorted by product tier. You will also find details for each vendor (Figure 3.4). **www.virtualmeetingsbook.com/vendors**.

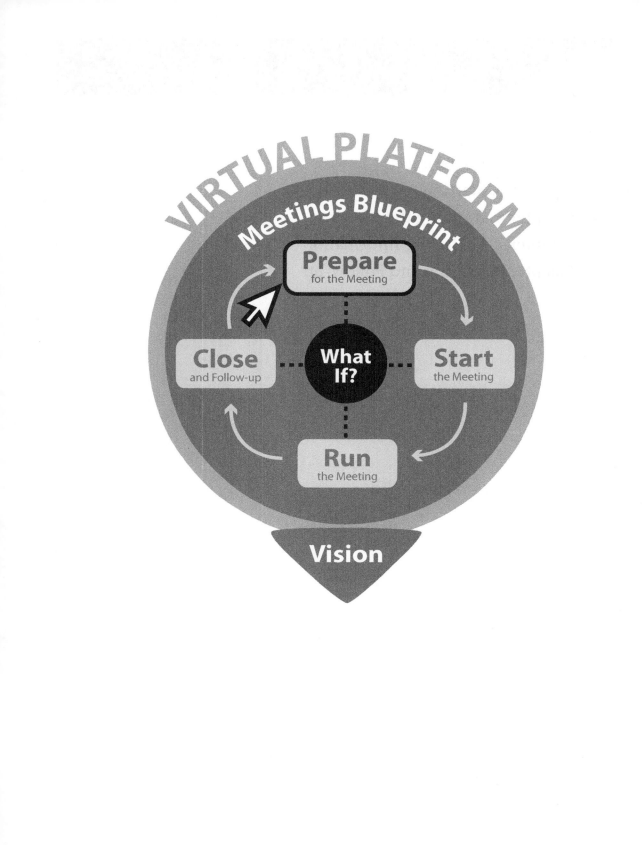

Preparing | 4

- The Virtual Dilemma
- Checklist for Preparing
- Decide the Meeting's Purpose
- Define the Meeting's Products
- Confirm That the Meeting Is Necessary
- Select the Participants
- Identify Probable Issues
- Develop the Process (Agenda)
- Choose the Virtual Platform
- Determine Key Methods and Timings
- Determine Meeting Rooms, Date, and Time
- Develop and Distribute the Meeting Notice
- Hold Preliminary Discussions as Needed
- Prepare the Virtual Meeting Room
- Select Your Ground Rules
- Prepare Your Roll Call List
- Prepare Your Opening Words
- Back to the Virtual Dilemma
- Summary: The Strategies for Preparing
- Virtual Resources for You

The Virtual Dilemma

It's been two weeks since your boss named you to lead the virtual team on improving the performance review process. The first team meeting is less than a week away. Unfortunately, given your other pressing responsibilities, you have not taken the time to prepare for the meeting. As you review your schedule, you find a single two-hour slot three days before the meeting that you could allocate to preparation. But you have two competing thoughts in particular that concern you.

- If this were an in-person first meeting, you figure you would need at least half of that time, if not all of it, to meet with your boss to make sure you understand her expectations, develop the agenda for the first meeting, assemble the information to send to people in advance, and book a room for the meeting. Well, at least you don't have to book the room.

- You are not familiar with any of the available virtual meeting tools. You've seen a few used before by others, and are pretty sure a tool would help with the group's focus and productivity—but you suspect that learning a new tool would eat up all your preparation time.

You are not sure which activity to prioritize.

With limited time to prepare for a virtual meeting, should I focus on learning how to use a virtual meeting tool or focus on figuring out what I want to get out of the meeting?

Far too many meetings fail due to lack of planning and preparation. This chapter provides a framework for planning a virtual meeting and includes a comprehensive list of the items to cover in preparing, as shown in Figure 4.1.

Note that not all items included in this chapter are needed for all virtual meetings. For example, the preparation you would do for a one-on-one meeting with a subordinate is not the same as the preparation required for a critical meeting with your supervisor and his or her boss to gain approval for a controversial initiative.

For the checklist, we have assumed that you are preparing for a critical meeting. Trim the list as needed for the meetings you commonly lead. The asterisked items (*) indicate those actions that every virtual meeting requires, regardless of its importance and number of participants. See the "Virtual Resources for You" section at the end of this chapter to download a copy of the preparation checklist.

Figure 4.1: Checklist for Preparing

❑ Decide the meeting's purpose.*
❑ Define the meeting's products.*
❑ Confirm that the meeting is necessary.*
❑ Select the participants.*
❑ Identify probable issues.*
❑ Develop the process (agenda).*
❑ Choose the virtual platform.*
❑ Determine key methods and timings.
❑ Determine meeting rooms, date, and time.*
❑ Develop and distribute the meeting notice.*
❑ Hold preliminary discussions beforehand, as needed.
❑ Prepare the virtual meeting room.*
❑ Select your ground rules.
❑ Prepare your roll call list of participants.
❑ Prepare your opening words.

* = Recommended for all meetings

Decide the Meeting's Purpose

Start planning for your virtual meeting by defining the six Ps of preparation: purpose, products, participants, probable issues, process, and platform. Purpose defines the overall goal to be achieved. To identify your meeting's purpose, consider the following questions:

- Why am I holding this meeting?
- At the meeting, what needs to be achieved?

Sample Purpose Statements

- To define the actions we will take to improve the performance review process
- To develop a strategic plan for the organization
- To ensure satisfactory progress is being made on a project

Define the Meeting's Products

The products are the specific items to be produced during the meeting that will define achievement of the purpose. Your desired products may cover one or more of what we call the three Hs. You will want to identify what you want people to have in their

- hands (deliverables),
- heads (knowledge), and
- hearts (beliefs).

To identify the products you want to result from the meeting, ask yourself one or more of the following questions:

- What specific tangible products or outcomes do I want to have produced when the meeting is over?
- When the meeting ends, what do I want the participants to have in their hands, heads, and hearts?
- Three months following the meeting, how will I know the meeting was successful?

Sample Products

- An action lists with the steps to be taken, by whom, and when
- A mission statement, guiding principles, broad goals, measurable targets, and specific strategies
- Approval to move forward and high expectations of success

Confirm That the Meeting Is Necessary

As indicated in Chapter 2, meetings, whether face-to-face or virtual, take time and tie up resources. Therefore, if a quality result can be achieved without holding a meeting, this is often preferred. To determine if a meeting is necessary, ask the following questions:

- What is my purpose in calling the meeting?
- What products should result from the meeting?
- Is it possible to achieve the purpose and products without a meeting?
- Are the purpose and products worth the time and resources that the meeting will consume?

Select the Participants

Who are the right participants for the virtual meeting? That depends on the meeting type.

Participants for a Status Meeting

- Those who need to know or their representatives

Participants for a Working Meeting

Each participant should

- understand the issue,
- have a stake in the outcome, and
- be empowered to make a decision or recommendation.

As a group, the participants should

- represent diverse communication styles,
- be knowledgeable about all relevant activities under study,
- be cross-functional and representative of all groups with a major stake in the outcome, and
- be drawn from various levels within the organization structure (e.g., managers, supervisors, and workers).

To help you identify the appropriate participants for a working meeting, consider the following questions:

- Who are the people who will be affected by the decision?
- What level of involvement should they have in the process?
- Whose perspectives, involvement, and buy-in are so critical that they should be at the table, or represented there?

Identify Probable Issues

Once you know the meeting's purpose, products, and participants, the next step is to identify the probable issues that might affect the meeting's success. Probable issues tend to fall into three different categories.

Categories of Probable Issues

- Topics: Questions and other items that the agenda will need to cover in order to create the products and achieve the meeting's purpose
- Ditches: Difficult items that must be addressed but can derail the meeting if not handled well
- Red Herrings: Items that are not directly related to the topic and should not be addressed, but which may come up

By identifying these issues ahead of time, you can make adjustments to the agenda and process you will use to achieve the meeting's purpose.

Sample Probable Issues

- How much is management willing to spend on improving the performance review process?

- How can we ensure that our compensation is competitive?

- How will we prevent favoritism and nepotism from biasing the performance reviews?

- Can technology be used to improve the way we do things?

- Is management really looking for a solution?

- Should the current pay-for-performance program be completely scrapped?

To identify probable issues, ask yourself or poll one or more attendees for answers to the questions that follow.

How to Identify Probable Issues

- What topics must be discussed to achieve the meeting's purpose and create the products?

- What questions or concerns will the participants have about the purpose or products?

- What potential ditches or red herrings might we encounter on our way to achieving the purpose and products?

- What other potential problems might surface and hinder us from achieving our purpose and products?

- How can we ensure that the meeting is not a waste of time?

Develop the Process (Agenda)

While purpose and products define the meeting's destination, the process or agenda is a roadmap for getting there. It identifies the steps needed to achieve the purpose and products, taking into account the participants and probable issues.

In this section, we have included several sample agendas that you might find helpful in developing your own agendas. See the "Virtual Resources for You" section at the end of this chapter for electronic copies of these agendas.

Choose the agenda that most closely represents your defined purpose and desired products. These agendas are adapted with permission from *The Secrets to Masterful Meetings.*[4]

Sample Agendas

- Issue Resolution
- Process Improvement
- Project Planning
- Status Meetings
- Strategic Planning
- Team Development

Issue Resolution

Purpose

- Define an issue; identify alternative solutions; or gain consensus on an alternative.

Products

- Selection criteria
- Alternative definitions
- Selected alternative and justification

Agenda

A. Getting started

B. What is the issue?

C. What criteria should we use in selecting a solution?

D. What are the alternatives?

E. What are the alternatives' strengths and weaknesses?

F. Are there other alternatives that combine key strengths?

G. Which alternative should we select?

H. Review and close.

Process Improvement

Purpose

- Define the changes necessary to increase the efficiency and effectiveness of a business process.

Products

- New process description
- Implementation plan

Agenda

A. Getting started

B. What are the process's overall goals?

C. How does the process work today?

D. What are the problems and root causes?

E. What are potential improvements?

F. How might we prioritize these improvements?

G. How will the new process work?

H. How will we implement this new process?

I. Review and close.

Project Planning

Purpose

- Identify the objectives of a project and the resources and timelines needed to complete it.

Product

- Project plan

Agenda

A. Getting started

B. Define the project's purpose and objectives.

C. Determine project's scope and products.

D. Identify critical success factors.

E. Develop an overall approach.

F. Define the resources, durations, dependencies, and schedule.

G. Identify risks and contingencies.

H. Review and close.

Status Meeting

Purpose

- Identify the status of a department, program, or project.

Products

- Updated status against plan
- Actions to be completed

Agenda

A. Getting started (one-minute check-in)

B. Remind participants of the overall department objectives.

C. Review and update the list of action items from a prior meeting.

D. Review the status by team: accomplishments, priorities for the next period, and issues for later discussion.

E. Prioritize discussion issues and allocate time.

F. Resolve issues.

G. Document action items for the next meeting.

H. Review and close.

Strategic Planning

Purpose

- Develop a shared vision and document the steps to achieve that vision.

Products

- Vision and mission statements
- Goals, objectives, and guiding principles
- Strategies and priorities

Agenda

A. Getting started

B. Review the situation analysis.

C. Develop the goals, mission, and vision.

D. Develop objectives.

E. Identify critical success factors and barriers.

F. Develop strategies and priorities.

G. Document action plans.

H. Review and close.

Team Development

Purpose

- Improve a team's ability to work together.

Products

- Team vision and team norms
- Our action plan
- Our monitoring plan and accountability plan

Agenda

A. Getting started

B.   What makes teams work?

C.   Develop our team vision.

D.   Define our issues and barriers.

E.   Identify strategies to achieve our vision.

F.   Develop our monitoring plan.

F.   Define our accountability plan.

G.   Review and close.

An Alternative Agenda Approach

The sample agendas indicate the purpose and products for the entire agenda. A different approach to agenda building is to indicate the purpose and desired outcome for each agenda item, as shown in Figure 4.2.

Figure 4.2: Purpose and Outcome by Agenda Item

Agenda Item	Purpose	Desired Outcome
Capital budget	Ensure that the capital budget is realistic and meets the needs of the organization.	Approval to proceed
Financial update	Report the current and projected financial condition.	Information only
JV partner candidates	Gain the board's input on potential partners in a joint venture.	List of potential partners

This detailed outcomes approach to agenda building is most helpful when there are numerous unrelated agenda items, and each item involves an independent product.

Customizing an Agenda

Once you have chosen an agenda to use as your starting point, you can customize the agenda to your particular situation based on your particular purpose, products, participants, and probable issues. Some examples follow.

Examples of How to Customize an Agenda

* For a meeting on improving the performance review process, you would likely use the process improvement agenda as your starting point. If you know that several

participants are heavily invested in the old process, you might include a new process step after Item B ("How does the process work today?") such as, "What are the strengths of the current process?"

- If you are putting together a project plan for implementing new customer-relationship-management software, you might be aware that the participants are concerned about a lack of management support for the project (i.e., a probable issue). Accordingly, you might include an Item H, "How do we ensure management buy-in?"

- The agenda should be designed to create an "opening-then-narrowing" experience for the participants.

  - Early parts of the process should open the participants to the possibilities of what could be done. During this segment, many potential approaches should be identified.

  - Later parts of the process should narrow the possibilities of what could be done, down to the strategies or recommendations that will be carried out.

Choose the Virtual Platform

The final "P" of the six Ps is to determine your virtual platform. Choose the platform that best supports the participants' executing the agenda and achieving the purpose and products. It should take into account the constraints on your time, your resources, and your skillset. See Chapter 3 for additional information on selecting the most appropriate platform to fit your needs.

Determine Key Methods and Timings

While the agenda defines what will happen in the meeting, the methods you choose will determine how each agenda item will be accomplished and the amount of time required to do so. In Chapter 8, you will find a detailed description of the following standard information gathering processes.

Sample Information Gathering Processes

- Brainstorming
- Grouping
- Listing
- Lobbying
- Polling
- Prioritizing
- Question and answer

- Round-robin
- Small group breakout
- The whip

Since one of the fundamental issues with virtual meetings is keeping people fully engaged and participating, we highly recommend that you plan a meaningful, interactive activity that engages all participants every ten to twenty minutes.

In this preparation step, think through how you will use the virtual platform for each agenda item by preparing a detailed agenda. The detailed agenda describes, for each agenda item, what information gathering process you will use and what features you will use in the virtual platform. We provide a sample detailed agenda for a meeting on performance reviews later in this chapter.

Estimating Timing

To estimate the duration for an agenda item, consider estimating the following:

- Introduction: How much time will it take to introduce the agenda item? Typically, this is one to five minutes, although some agenda introductions might take more time.
- Unit time: How much time will it take to process one item? Typically this is one to ten minutes. For example, identifying each step in the performance review process might require only two minutes each.
- Number of units: How many items will likely be identified? Let's assume for our example that we will have twenty steps in the performance review process.
- Wrap-up: How much time will it take to wrap up the discussion after all items have been identified? Let's assume that it will take another five minutes.

The mathematical formula for calculating the amount of time is as follows:

Time for an Agenda Item
Introduction + (Number of units x Unit time) + Wrap-up

For our example above, the amount of time required would be calculated as follows: Time = 5 + (20 steps x 2) + 5 = 50 minutes.

Sample Detailed Agenda

What follows is a sample detailed agenda process. The "Virtual Details" section describes how the meeting leader will use the virtual platform to execute each agenda item. *Note that this is an agenda for a series of meetings. We typically recommend that no one virtual meeting last more than two hours without a substantial break.*

Figure 4.3: Sample Detailed Agenda

Meeting	Performance Review Process: Team Meetings
Purpose	**Products**
To define the actions we will take to improve the performance review process	Description of the proposed performance review process Implementation plan

Preparation

- PowerPoint
- Goals of the process and current process steps gained through pre-session interviews
- Problems (20 rectangles) and root causes (8 circles)
- Microsoft Word document
- Parking boards: issues list, decisions list, action plan table
- Recommendations to the process goals and current process steps
- Whiteboards:
  - Key topics
  - Process strengths
  - Potential improvements (whiteboard divided by root cause)
- Voting tool to load with improvements

A. Getting started	
Process	List the key topics participants want to discuss; group the topics into categories.
Virtual Details	• Have participants record their key topics on the whiteboard. • Move items on whiteboard into groups.
Timing	10 minutes (2 + (12 issues x 0.5) + 2)

B. What are the overall goals of the process and how does the process work today?

Process	Present the current process goals and steps; provide an update based on the recommendations.
Virtual Details	• Have goals and steps listed in PowerPoint based on pre-session interviews. • Share it to the desktop so all can view it. • With the current goals and process in one half of the screen, use a round-robin and collect recommended additions, changes, and deletions (record this in Word in the second panel of the screen). • After collecting all changes, review each one and ask if there is any disagreement. If not, make the change; if so, use the informed majority process to resolve it.
Timing	45 minutes (10 + (6 changes x 5) + 5)

C. What are the strengths of the current process?

Process	Brainstorm strengths.
Virtual Details	• Use the whiteboard to collect strengths. • Invite people to put a "ditto" mark next to a strength if they agree with something that has previously been said.
Timing	10 minutes (2 + (12 strengths x 0.5) + 2)

D. What are the problems and root causes?

Process	Have the team list problems with the process and then group the problems based on common root causes.
Virtual Details	• In advance, have a PowerPoint slide with approximately 20 rectangles (problems) and 8 circles (root causes). • Use desktop sharing to show the PowerPoint. Use a round-robin activity to collect problems. Type each problem into a rectangle as it is being said. • Once all problems are identified, go back and review each one, asking, "Why does this occur?" Using the drawing tool, connect each problem to one or more root causes.
Timing	60 minutes (5 + (12 problems x 4) + 7)

E. What are potential improvements?

Process	Brainstorm ways to improve the process with a special focus on addressing the root causes.
Virtual Details	• In advance, divide the whiteboard into sections, with a section for each root cause. • Give the format (verb–object–purpose) for potential improvements and type an example in one of the whiteboard sections. • Give brainstorming instructions and have participants record responses.
Timing	15 minutes (2 + (20 improvements x 0.5) + 3)

F. How might we prioritize these improvements?

Process	Combine improvements where appropriate, and use informed majority to vote on each potential improvement.
Virtual Details	• With the improvements still on the whiteboard, review each one. • Indicate you need a "sponsor" of each improvement to speak for it, and someone to speak against it. Have each person present a case, and then ask for other comments. • Use the voting tool to vote on the improvement. Move on to the next. • If no one wants to serve as sponsor for an improvement, it gets eliminated; if no one speaks against the improvement, it is automatically accepted and no vote is held. • Place an asterisk on the improvements that will be implemented.
Timing	70 minutes (5 + (20 improvements x 3) + 5)

G. How will the new process work?

Process	Assuming that the improvements are implemented, use a listing activity to get the group to update the original process flow with the new process flow.

Virtual Details	• Using desktop sharing and PowerPoint, ask the sponsor of each accepted improvement to identify how the process will change based on the improvement.
	• Make the changes in PowerPoint.
Timing	75 minutes (5 + (8 improvements x 8) + 6)

H. How will we implement this new process?	
Process	List the action steps necessary to implement the new process.
Virtual Details	• Have a Word action plan table developed in advance.
	• Using desktop sharing and the action plan table, ask the sponsor of each accepted improvement to identify the one to three steps necessary to implement the improvement, and then record it in the table.
	• Ask who should implement each action, and then ask that person, if present, to provide a date for completing the action.
Timing	30 minutes (3 + (8 improvements x 3) + 3)

I. Review and close.	
Process	Review the work that was done; review the parking boards; evaluate the session; discuss the next steps; and close the session.
Virtual Details	• Prepare in advance a Word document for the issues list and decisions lists, as well as the action plan table described above.
	• As the meeting progresses, record issues, decisions, and actions in the document (while in desktop sharing mode, if appropriate).
	• Read through the issues, decisions, and actions lists before closing the meeting.
Timing	15 minutes (3 + (10 items x 1) + 2)

See the "Virtual Resources for You" section at the end of this chapter to obtain a template you can use to create a detailed agenda.

Determine Meeting Rooms, Date, and Time

When there are multiple people from the same location attending a virtual meeting, we recommend that they assemble in the same room during the meeting. Having people physically together, even in a virtual meeting, has two important advantages:

- They can hold one another accountable in staying focused and avoiding the temptation to multitask.
- They can interact with one another more easily, read body language, and respond more appropriately.

Depending upon the number of people in the same location, the physical meeting room can be a conference room or even one of the participants' offices.

Meeting Date and Time

There are several factors to consider when deciding the date and time for a meeting. The list below is a starting point, ordered by relative importance. The items on the list and the order may vary for your situation.

Factors to Consider When Defining Date and Time

- When must the results of the meeting be known?
- Who are the people critical to the success of the meeting? And what are their available times?
- What date and time are convenient for you?

Date, Times, and Locations to Avoid

Avoid	Reason
Meeting on Monday morning or Friday afternoon	People may be distracted from the weekend that is coming or the one that has just passed.
Meeting the day before a holiday or the day after a holiday	People may be distracted by the holiday that is coming or the one that has just passed.
Starting a meeting right after lunch	People tend to be more sluggish and have low energy and creativity.
Locations where participants can be distracted by activity outside the room	Outside activity may reduce meeting productivity.
Rooms that are too small or too large for the audience	Participants may be negatively affected by the environment.

Develop and Distribute the Meeting Notice

The meeting notice defines the key information that participants need in order to come to the meeting prepared and ready to work. If possible, distribute the meeting notice at least a week prior to the meeting. What are the appropriate contents for a meeting notice?

Contents of the Meeting Notice

- Meeting purpose, expected products, and proposed agenda
- Link to the virtual platform
- Gathering time, and start and end times
- Invited attendees
- Recommended items to bring

Figure 4.4 provides a sample meeting notice for the performance review improvement team.

For recurring meetings such as status meetings, the meeting notice may not be necessary if the same items are covered in every meeting with the same virtual platform link. For other meetings, the meeting notice may be verbal (e.g., voicemail) or in writing. See the "Virtual Resources for You" section at the end of this chapter for a meeting notice template.

To help in starting the meeting on time, make the first time on the agenda the gathering time followed by the actual start time. In this way, participants will know that they are expected to arrive early so that the meeting can start on time. If there are items for participants to review or actions that need to be taken prior to the meeting, distribute these beforehand, as well.

Figure 4.4: Sample Meeting Notice

The Performance Review Improvement Team
xx/xx/xx Gather 8:50 ET / End 11:00 ET
1st Meeting
Be sure to access the link about 10 minutes before the start of the meeting.

Use the following link for the meeting: www.k1fasf.biz/179avads121.

If this will be your first time using the virtual meeting platform, please try the link at least twenty-four hours in advance to ensure there are no technical problems. If you need assistance before or during the meeting, contact our moderator, Jim Hamilton, at 770-555-1440.

Meeting's Purpose
  • To kick off the virtual team on improving the performance review process

Expected Products
  • Definition of success, group norms, work process, meetings and logistics plan, communications plan

Proposed Agenda
  8:50 Gather
  9:00 Start
  A. Welcome, purpose, charge, deliverables, meeting purpose
  B. Key topics
  C. Agenda
  D. Meeting ground rules
  E. Gifts and hooks
  F. Our definition of success
  G. Proposed work process
  H. Team norms
  I. Operating logistics
  J. Review and next steps
  K. Evaluation and Close
  11:00 End

Invited Attendees
  ☐ Kathy K. —Team Leader
  ☐ Cleve C.—Documenter   ☐ Ken M.
  ☐ Bill G.   ☐ Vanessa R.
  ☐ Trina J.   ☐ Andrea T.

In Advance: Review the team charter sent to you last week. Identify any specific meeting issues you would like to see addressed.

Bring to the Meeting: The team charter and your list of issues

Hold Preliminary Discussions as Needed

For critical or controversial meetings, it may be important to hold preliminary discussions with one or more participants before the meeting. The list below provides a sampling of reasons to hold these preliminary discussions.

Hold Discussions Prior to the Meeting If . . .

- the issues are complex, and it would be helpful to have a small group create a starting-point solution;

- a critical mass is needed to move a decision forward, and you want to seek an initial agreement from a core group;

- one or more of the decision-makers have an inadequate understanding of the issue, and these misunderstandings could prevent a successful meeting;

- one or more participants stand to lose something if the meeting is successful, and therefore should understand in advance what might happen in the meeting;

- one or more participants tend to point out problems, and it would be helpful to get them focused on seeking solutions; or

- one or more participants may attempt to change the agenda to address their personal issues.

Prepare the Virtual Meeting Room

Whatever tool you select, consider the following to help ensure you are fully versed in it. (Adapted with permission from *Challenges of Virtual and Blended Meetings*, by Rachel Smith, director of digital facilitation services, the Grove Consultants International.)

- Spend time practicing with the technology before the meeting. Be sure to load any files you will be showing and to run through all the tools and options you think you might use. Consider practicing using two computers, one showing what the meeting leader will see and one showing what a participant will see; it will help confirm what you and the participants will experience.

- Offer to give a brief orientation session to participants in advance of the meeting to increase the level of comfort for those who are unfamiliar with the technology. The orientation session can also serve to identify potential technology problems early.

- If possible, arrange to have someone on hand during the session to serve in the moderator role to answer technical questions and help attendees who get stuck. Having a moderator working with you to handle technical issues will allow you to keep the meeting running smoothly while your moderator assists attendees in trouble.

- Ask attendees who are calling in from their computers to use a headset or earphones. When people don't use a headset or earphones, their computer microphone can sometimes pick up the output from the speakers and broadcast it back into the conference. While the offender often can't hear this, others on the call will likely find the feedback or echoes unpleasant.

- If some people simply can't use a headset or earphones, ask them to keep their microphone muted unless they are speaking.

Select Your Ground Rules

Ground rules provide a vehicle for gaining agreement on a set of behaviors that will guide how participants should interact with one another. While some teams may have worked together for some time and have established their own functional, unspoken ground rules, we have found that most groups benefit from a deliberate process of identifying in-bounds and out-of-bounds behavior.

Consider ground rules that guide what people do (procedural) and how they do it (behavioral). Some sample ground rules are as follows.

Sample Ground Rules

- Start and end on time.
- Everyone speaks.
- Have one conversation.
- Use the parking boards.
- No beeps, buzzes, or ringy-dingies.
- Do meeting work only.
- Take a stand.

- Use ELMO–Enough, Let's Move On.
- Be soft on people and hard on ideas.
- Give benefits first.
- Share all relevant information.[5]
- Discuss un-discussable issues.[6]
- Explain reasoning and intent.[7]

Special Ground Rules for Virtual Meetings

Consider adding specific ground rules to assist with virtual meeting etiquette, such as the following.

- Announce yourself when joining the meeting and inform the group if you are leaving the meeting early.

- Always identify yourself before speaking.

- Avoid using the "hold" button, especially when music or other sounds result.

- Stay 100 percent focused during the meeting; avoid doing other work, answering e-mails, etc.

Prepare Your Roll Call List

During the virtual meeting, you will frequently invite each person to speak on a topic. It is helpful to use the same order each time. Accordingly, prepare a list of participants and locations.

- Considering placing the names in alphabetical order by first name. This will help the participants recognize when their turn to speak is coming.

- If most of the people are in one location, have the people in all other locations listed alphabetically first, followed by an alphabetical list of those in the primary location.

- If there are several locations with multiple people, consider listing the locations alphabetically, and listing the people alphabetically in each location.

Prepare Your Opening Words

The final step in preparation is to prepare the words you will say to open the meeting. At the beginning of the meeting, you will want to thank, inform, excite, and empower. The next chapter provides details on these critical points.

Back to the Virtual Dilemma

Let's return to the question posed by the virtual dilemma that started this chapter.

> **With limited time to prepare for a virtual meeting, should I focus on learning how to use a virtual meeting tool or focus on figuring out what I want to get out of the meeting?**

Perhaps at this point, the answer is much more obvious. Recall that you are unfamiliar with virtual meeting technology, and you only have a two-hour slot three days before the meeting in order to complete all of your preparation.

Given the information from this chapter, it could easily require two hours or more to fully prepare to ensure the meeting is effective, productive and engaging. Accordingly, if you choose to use virtual meeting technology to assist with the meeting, we recommend you choose the simplest applications that offer desktop sharing as their primary feature (see Chapter 3). While these technologies are not as feature-rich as some of the other virtual platforms, they are often the easiest to learn.

Summary: The Strategies for Preparing

In summary, the strategies for preparing for *masterful virtual meetings* include the following:

Strategy 12.   For your meeting, define the six Ps of preparation: purpose, products, participants, probable issues, process, and platform.

Strategy 13.   Design an agenda to achieve the purpose and products, taking into account the participants and probable issues.

Strategy 14.   Prepare a detailed agenda that describes how you will use the virtual meeting platform to execute each agenda item.

Strategy 15.   Use a variety of information gathering processes to make the meeting interesting and engaging.

Strategy 16.   Distribute a meeting notice in advance of the meeting to notify participants of the meeting's purpose and the virtual meeting access link, and to encourage participants to prepare for the meeting.

Strategy 17.   Be sure that the first time appearing on the meeting notice is the gathering time—not the start time.

Strategy 18.   Hold preliminary discussions with people if the meeting is critical or includes controversial topics.

Virtual Resources for You

The following resources are available on the Virtual Meetings Website to aid you in implementing the strategies in this chapter.

In our tools library, you will find the following:
- Preparation checklist
- Sample agendas
- Detailed agenda template
- Meeting notice template

www.virtualmeetingsbook.com/tools

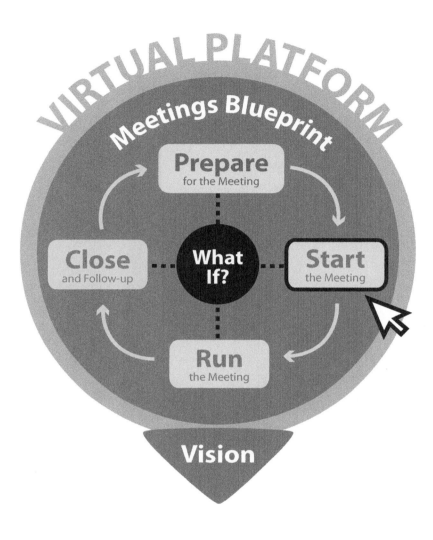

- The Virtual Dilemma
- Checklist for Starting
- Minimize the Impact of Technical Issues
- Start the Meeting on Time
- Deliver Your Opening Statement
- Perform a Roll Call
- Engage Participants (The Great Starting Question)
- Confirm the Agenda
- Review the Ground Rules
- Review the Parking Boards
- Make Introductions, If Needed
- Summary: The Strategies for Starting
- Virtual Resource for You

The Virtual Dilemma

Your virtual meeting is scheduled to start promptly at 9:00 a.m. As you requested, all eighteen of the people you invited for the meeting have attempted to log-in ten minutes ahead of time to download the software so that they would be in the virtual meeting room by the meeting's start.

Unfortunately, only fifteen of the eighteen were successful at logging in. At 8:53 you get a call from one person who can't get the software to download. You begin troubleshooting with this person when, at 8:57, another call comes in from someone whose firewall won't permit access to the software. You ask this second person to hold while you go back to the first person. By 9:02 you have solved the download problem and you quickly post a message that the meeting will be starting in just a few minutes due to technical problems. You are about to focus your attention on the firewall problem when a third call comes in. This person explains that she is using a computer that is running a different operating system than most and that the operating system doesn't seem to be compatible with the virtual meeting software. By 9:06 you convince that person to find another machine to use in the office, which allows you to talk with the person with the firewall problem. By 9:11, all problems are resolved and you are ready to start the meeting— except three people who didn't experience problems have dropped off because they got tired of waiting!

How do you prevent this from happening to you?

How a virtual meeting starts often sets participants' expectations for everything that follows. Start well and you create an expectation that the meeting will be engaging, effective, and well worth the time. Start poorly, however, and you can lose participants even before you get to the first agenda item.

A meeting's start includes all the activities done before addressing the first work item on the agenda. Let's begin with the checklist for starting, Figure 5.1.

Figure 5.1: Checklist for Starting

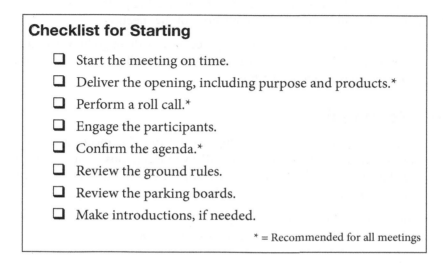

Checklist for Starting

❑ Start the meeting on time.

❑ Deliver the opening, including purpose and products.*

❑ Perform a roll call.*

❑ Engage the participants.

❑ Confirm the agenda.*

❑ Review the ground rules.

❑ Review the parking boards.

❑ Make introductions, if needed.

* = Recommended for all meetings

The opening can take as little as five minutes and as long as forty-five minutes or more depending on the size of the group and the steps you use. You should adjust the list as needed for the meetings you lead. Those items asterisked (*) should be done in every meeting, regardless of the meeting's importance or number of participants. See the "Virtual Resource for You" section at the end of this chapter to download a copy of the starting checklist.

Minimize the Impact of Technical Issues

With virtual meetings, the start of a meeting is doubly important. As demonstrated in the virtual dilemma at the beginning of this chapter, a well-planned virtual meeting can be completely derailed due to technology issues. While it is nearly impossible to avoid all technical issues all the time, there are strategies you can use to minimize their impact.

Strategies to Minimize Technical Issues and Their Impact

- Ask people to access the virtual meeting platform at least ten minutes ahead of the start of the meeting.

- For those who will be using the virtual meeting platform for the first time, encourage them to test the link at least twenty-four hours in advance to ensure there are no technical problems.

- If you are expecting more than three or four other people in the virtual meeting, assign someone not participating in the meeting to serve as the moderator, or technical assistant, whose role it is to resolve any technical issues that you or a participant might have.

- Include the name and telephone number of the moderator in the meeting notice.

- If this is the first time you are using the virtual meeting platform, be sure to test all the features you will be using well in advance of the meeting.

- Plan your setup time so that you are prepared and ready to go between fifteen and thirty minutes prior to the start of the meeting. This will give you extra time in case you encounter unexpected difficulties.

Start the Meeting on Time

Among meeting leaders, a common challenge is getting the meeting started on time. Unfortunately, most leaders "punish the punctual" by making those who arrive on time wait for those who are late. In some organizations, punishing the punctual is such a cultural norm that virtual meeting participants habitually arrive late to avoid "being punished."

Of course, it can be difficult to start a meeting when key participants are tardy. Consider the following strategies to develop a culture of starting meetings on time.

Strategies for Starting on Time

- Get permission in advance from all participants to start the meeting at the appointed time.

- Make sure the meeting notice gives a gathering time and a start time. Most people pay attention to the first time they see.

- Consider setting the start time for meetings for five minutes after the hour or half-hour to allow people leaving an earlier meeting time to arrive punctually at yours.

- If someone else other than you will kick off the meeting, make sure he or she is aware of this role and that the two of you have agreed upon the time.

- Consider gaining the group's agreement on a suitable penalty for arriving late, such as a five-dollar donation to the party pool.

Deliver Your Opening Statement

Whether in virtual meetings or face-to-face ones, meeting leaders often start by reviewing the agenda—if they have one—and diving straight into the first agenda item. As a result, participants often aren't sure of the meeting's purpose, its intended products, why the meeting is beneficial, or why the meeting should be important to them. In essence, meetings often begin with an ineffective start that can hurt the rest of the meeting.

Your opening words must set the tone, pace, and expectations for the meeting. Through the opening, you must convey your vision of the meeting and the benefit to be gained. What should you say to make the opening effective?

Items to Cover in Your Opening Statement

- **Thank** the participants for coming.

- **Inform** them about the overall purpose of the meeting and the products that will result.

- **Excite** the participants by providing a vision of success and the benefits to them. Use the words "you" or "your" at least four times to ensure that you describe the benefits to them.

- **Empower** them by identifying the authority they have been given, the important role they play in the process, or the reason they were selected for the meeting.

Opening with Energy

How you deliver the opening is also important. When a leader speaks in a low monotone with little or no expression, participants get the message that the leader has limited interest in the meeting and low confidence that the meeting will achieve results. When the meeting leader speaks with excitement, interest, and passion about a topic, this feeling is conveyed to the participants.

Depending upon your virtual meeting platform, the participants may not be able to see you, so it is even more important in virtual meetings that you convey energy, interest, and excitement when you speak. Most of us, when we are in casual conversation, speak at what we call Level 1 energy: just loud enough, and with just enough energy, to keep people awake. Unfortunately, when we are leading a meeting over a period of time, our energy level drops and we might put people to sleep! When leading virtual meetings (and face-to-face meetings, as well), consider raising your energy two levels to Level 3. Start the meeting at Level 3, as shown in Figure 5.2, and this energy level will likely spill over to energize the topic and the participants.

Figure 5.2: Level 3 Energy

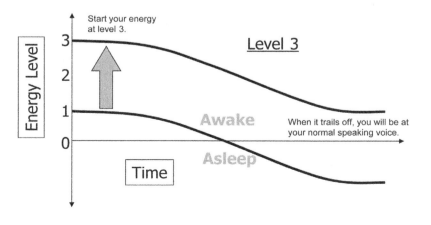

Along with using Level 3 energy, consider delivering the opening in the following way.

Delivering the Opening Words

- Sit tall; don't slouch.
- Speak loudly, clearly, and with expression in your voice.
- Vary your tone.
- Use pauses for emphasis.
- Avoid speaking too fast or too slow.
- Be animated, using defined gestures.
- Avoid filler words (e.g., ah, er, and um).
- If appropriate, make eye contact by looking directly at the camera while you are delivering your opening.

When you deliver the opening in this way, and the opening incorporates the items we discussed earlier, the participants are more likely to understand why they are there, capture your vision and excitement about the meeting, and understand the role they play and the benefit to them. What follows is a sample opening.

Sample Opening Words

- I want to **thank** you all for agreeing to be a part of this meeting.
- Let me start by **informing** you about why we are here.
    - As you all know, we've been having significant difficulty with our performance review process.
    - There have been reports of wide differences among our departments on what is considered "meets" versus "exceeds" versus "far exceeds" expectations. A number of employees have commented that the review process is all about how well you are liked and not how well you perform. Additionally, we have had cases of people given high ratings just a few months before being fired for poor performance. In summary, it doesn't appear that our performance review process is effective.
    - We have been called together to create a new process that will alleviate concerns like these.
- Why is this **exciting**?
    - If we are successful, and if we do our job well, it will result in a process that you and your people can believe in, have faith in, and feel motivated by. And if your people are motivated, you know that it makes your job so

much easier: fewer problems, fewer complaints, better morale, and better performance—and a better bottom line means better bonuses for you, me, and everyone in the organization.

- In addition, if we do our jobs well, you will have the thanks and gratitude of the senior staff and your peers for the significant improvements you will have made.

- I want to make sure you know that you have been **empowered** to get this job done.

  - Each of you was handpicked by the Leadership Team to be part of this process.

  - They believe you have the knowledge as well as the vision for creating a much better process.

  - They are looking forward to your recommendations.

Perform a Roll Call

After delivering your opening statement, perform a roll call by saying the names of the people present on the call and their location, and asking them to acknowledge by saying something such as, "Yes, I'm here." The purpose of the roll call is to ensure that you are aware of everyone who is on the call and for people to begin connecting voices to names. After saying all the names believed to be on the call, be sure to ask if anyone is present who wasn't named. If so, update your list accordingly.

Your virtual meeting software may be able to assist you with the roll call by displaying a list of people who are on the call. Otherwise you may use a list such as the one shown in Figure 5.3, which has check boxes you can use to indicate the participants who have responded to a question.

Figure 5.3: List of Participants for the Roll Call

						Andrea, Atlanta
						Bill, Boston
						Cleve, Chicago
						Ken, Dallas
						Trina, Denver
						Vanessa, San Diego
						Kathy, Atlanta (project manager)

Assign Your Eyes in the Room If Appropriate

For each location with multiple people, it is often helpful to assign a person as your "eyes in the room." Empower these people with the responsibility to stop you—in mid-sentence if necessary—anytime they detect that you need to speed up because people in the room seem to be disengaging, to slow down because people appear to be lost, to alert you anytime a hand is raised and you don't "see" it, or to point out any other group behavior that requires a response. Consider giving permission to all others to do the same, as well.

Engage Participants (The Great Starting Question)

After delivering the opening and the roll call, consider getting the participants immediately engaged. This engagement step involves everyone quickly and prepares them for the rest of the meeting.

How do you engage participants early in a virtual meeting? For some teams, it is best to start with a question that is focused on the task at hand. For other teams, it may be more appropriate to start with a question that focuses on people. We recommend any one of the following:

Sample Initial Engagement Approaches

- Key Topics Approach
    - Think about the meeting purpose.
    - If we are going to accomplish this purpose, there are probably specific topics that you know we need to cover, specific issues that we have to address, or maybe specific ideas that we should discuss.
    - Let's build the list. If we are going to be successful today, what topics do we need to talk about?

- Personal Outcomes Approach
    - Let's assume this meeting was highly successful.
    - Think about the things that resulted, the outcomes that occurred, and the things that would make you say, "This was a great meeting."
    - Let's build the list. Given our purpose and products, what are the outcomes you personally would like to see come out of today's meeting?

- One-Minute Check-In Approach
    - It has been several days since we were all together. Let's start with each person giving a quick, one-minute check-in.
    - We were last together on [date]. Since that time, there probably have been one or more significant events that have occurred in your personal or professional life.

- Consider the major events that have occurred and pick one that was significant for you. Let's go through the roll call list. What is a significant event that has happened to you since we were last together?

Great Starting Questions

Each of the alternatives above is phrased to help participants visualize their answers by using a format known as the starting question.[8] To construct a great starting question, use the three steps that follow:

- Start with an image building phrase (e.g., "Think about . . . Imagine . . . Consider . . . If . . .").

- Extend the image so the participants can visualize their answers. This usually takes two or three additional phrases.

- Ask the direct question that you want answered.

When you ask questions in this way, participants typically visualize their answers and are immediately able to respond. If you simply ask the direct question (e.g., "What is a significant event that has happened to you since we were last together?"), participants tend to become silent as they try to visualize answers. This kind of silence can significantly reduce the energy and can indirectly disempower the participants by giving them the sense that they are incapable of responding to your questions. With a great starting question, however, you help them to identify their answers quickly by providing an image that helps them "see" their answers.

You should use great starting questions at the beginning of a meeting to engage participants, and also at any time you want them to provide a lot of responses, such as when identifying steps in a process, brainstorming potential strategies, and listing alternatives. Figure 5.4 includes samples of direct questions and the much better starting question.

Figure 5.4: Sample Starting Questions

Direct Question	Sample Starting Question
How does the performance review process work today; what are the steps?	I would like to build a list of the steps in the current performance review process. Imagine that you have a great employee who performs extremely well year after year, and you want to make sure you cover all the bases in the performance review process to ensure that she receives a very positive review. Think about all the steps that you or she would have to take as part of the performance review process, all the things that would have to be done early in the year, late in the year, etc. Let's build the list. What are the steps in our current performance review process?
What are the problems with the current process?	Think about our last performance review cycle. Consider the things that were real problems, the things that frustrated you, the things that worked very poorly, or the things that were just real problems. Think about the things that made you say, "There's got to be a better way to do this!" What are some of those frustrating problems with the current performance review process?
What are things we could do to improve the current process?	We are ready to build a list of things to do to improve the performance review process. Look over the problems we need to fix. Consider things we could do to solve them. Think about things you have seen implemented in other places. Consider how technology might be used to improve the performance review process or ways that we can better organize to get the work done. Let your mind see all the possibilities that we might consider. Let's list some of the ideas that could be put in place to improve our process. Who wants to start?

Tips for Using the Initial Engagement Approach

There are several techniques that can help you be more effective with the initial engagement approach.

- Name the person who will go first before you ask the question. As a result, this person will listen much more closely and be better prepared to answer.

- Give the participants about a minute to jot down their responses before the first person responds. This way, people will have an opportunity to listen to the person speaking rather than be distracted by their own thoughts of what they will say.

- Use a round-robin approach by starting with the first person and going through the roll call list. Round-robins avoid the awkward silence when people don't know who should go next.

- If you ask for personal outcomes or key topics, consider recording the responses in a document or having participants record their responses on a whiteboard. You will be able to come back to the information after confirming the agenda. Figure 5.5 provides an example of participants recording key topics on a whiteboard.

Figure 5.5: Key Topics Recorded on a Whiteboard

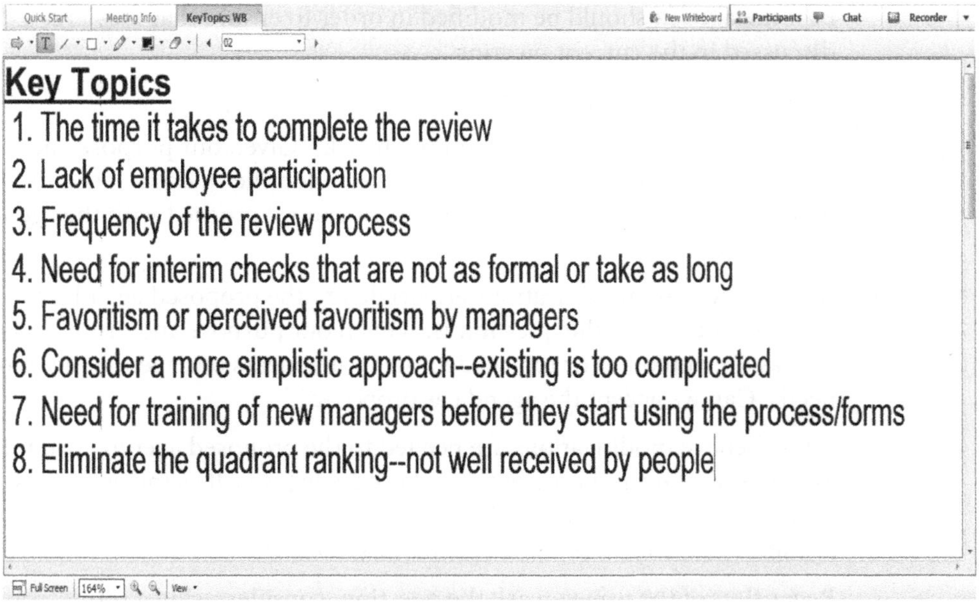

Confirm the Agenda

After completing the opening statement and engaging the participants, the next step is to review the agenda and time limits, if appropriate. The purpose of the review is to ensure that the participants understand how the meeting will flow and to gain confirmation that the agenda will address the purpose and products identified in the opening. To confirm the agenda, consider the following steps.

Steps to Confirm the Agenda[9]

- In the agenda review, consider covering the steps that will be taken, the products that will be created, and the timeframe for each step.

- Indicate how each step contributes to the overall meeting purpose.

- If you asked for personal outcomes or key topics as an initial engagement strategy, you can use the results to confirm the agenda.

    - After reviewing the agenda, review each personal outcome or key topic listed.

    - Ask the participants to identify under which agenda item each outcome or topic will likely be covered.

    - Circle any outcome or topic not covered by the proposed agenda.

    - After reviewing all outcomes or topics, go back to those circled items.

    - Determine with the group whether these will be saved for a later meeting or if the agenda should be modified in order to ensure that they are discussed in the current meeting.

- Ask the participants to confirm the agenda.

    - To ask the question neutrally, you might ask, "Given our purpose and products [as well as the outcomes or topics identified], do we need to make any modifications to the agenda, or can we proceed with the agenda as proposed?"

    - If you believe no modifications are needed to the proposed agenda, a different way to ask the question is: "Given our purpose and products [as well as the outcomes or topics identified], it appears our agenda meets our needs. Can we accept the agenda as proposed?"

    - If you believe modifications are needed to the proposed agenda, you might ask instead, "Given our purpose and products [as well as the outcomes or topics identified], I would like to propose just a few changes to the agenda…. Can we accept the agenda as amended?"

    - Regardless of the way you ask the question, consider using a round-robin to get everyone's feedback.

    - If other modifications are requested, you will be able to use the consensus building strategies described in Chapter 10.

Figure 5.6 provides a sample of how the key topics are annotated to indicate where in the agenda each will be covered.

Figure 5.6: Key Topics Annotated with Agenda References

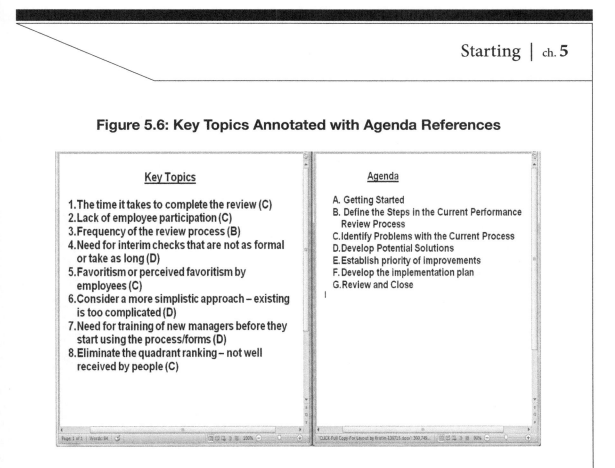

Review the Ground Rules

As indicated in Chapter 4, ground rules provide a vehicle for gaining agreement on a set of behaviors that will guide how participants should interact with one another. During preparation you will have selected the ground rules to use. During your opening, you will review the ground rules as follows.

Steps in Reviewing Ground Rules

- If this is the first meeting of the team, review and explain each ground rule.

- If the team meets frequently, it may be adequate just to remind the team of the ground rules without reviewing each one.

- If the group has a frequent dysfunction (e.g., interrupting one another), consider adding a ground rule to address it (e.g., no interruptions).

Over time, ground rules can help team members become self-correcting. They will begin policing themselves based on the ground rules that they have established and reinforced. Figure 5.7 provides a sample list of ground rules.

Figure 5.7: Sample Ground Rules

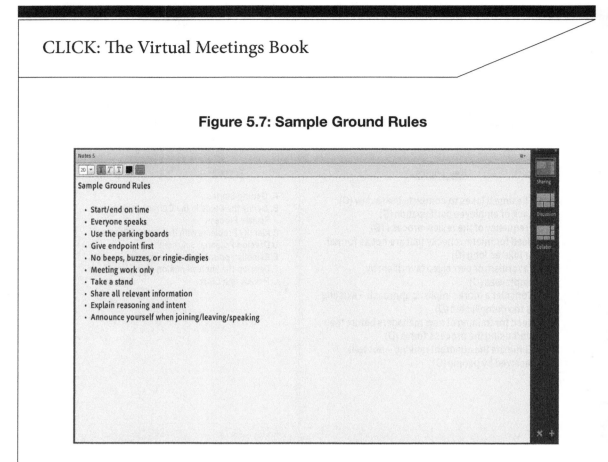

Recharge Ground Rule?

In face-to-face meetings that last a day or longer, we often ask participants to establish a "recharge" ground rule that the team will perform if energy begins to wane. A recharge combines something you do with your voice and body, and can't last more than fifteen seconds. As examples, teams have chosen such recharges as the chicken dance, the wave, the hokey pokey, and the "YMCA."

In virtual meetings, however, we recommend keeping meeting segments to no more than two hours and having at least a thirty-minute break between segments to allow participants to recharge. Therefore, we do not typically introduce a recharge activity as part of the ground rules for virtual meetings.

Review the Parking Boards

During a meeting, people will often bring up topics that are not directly related to the meeting's purpose or topics, but will be covered in a later agenda item. Additionally, there will be times during the meeting that decisions will be made or follow-up actions identified. In each of these cases, consider "parking" the information in a document so that everyone is aware of it.

For most meetings, we find three parking boards are particularly useful. At the beginning of the meeting, quickly review the purpose of the parking boards.

Three Common Parking Boards

- Issues list: Topics that need to be discussed later in the meeting or entirely outside the meeting

- Decisions list: Decisions made by the group that should be documented for future reference

- Actions list: Actions to be performed sometime after the completion of the meeting

Make Introductions, If Needed

If the meeting includes people who don't know one another, introductions may be appropriate. There are two types of introductions that we recommend, depending upon the situation.

Short-Form Introductions

- Ask people to share their name, organization, and role.

- If most people generally know one another, but there are a few who don't, consider just the short form.

Long-Form Introductions

- The long form is appropriate when the participants generally don't know one another.

- Ask the participants to identify their name, organization, role, and one specific outcome or key topic most important to them.

- With the long form, consider recording the questions on the screen to ensure that people understand what they are being asked to say.

- Give participants time to write down their thoughts before the first person speaks.

- Set a time limit for each introduction (e.g., thirty seconds); consider using a clock with an alarm as a reminder of the time.

Summary: The Strategies for Starting

In summary, the strategies for starting virtual meetings effectively include the following:

Strategy 19. Ask people to access the virtual meeting platform at least ten minutes before the meeting is supposed to start.

Strategy 20. If you are expecting more than three or four other people in the virtual meeting, assign someone not participating in the meeting to serve as the moderator, or technical assistant, whose role it is to be the point of contact for resolving any technical issues that you or a participant might have.

Strategy 21.   Achieve an on-time start by making the first time on the agenda the gathering time and gaining advance permission to start on time.

Strategy 22.   Deliver a strong, effective opening by:

- thanking the participants for coming,
- informing them of the purpose and desired products,
- exciting them about the benefits to them, and
- empowering them by identifying the authority they have been given and role they play.

Strategy 23.   To ensure that you are aware of everyone who is on the call and to allow people to begin connecting voices to names, perform a roll call with names and location, and ask each person to acknowledge with a, "Yes, I'm here."

Strategy 24.   For each location with multiple people, assign a person as your "eyes in the room" to alert you when you need to slow down, speed up, or take an alternative action based on what is happening in the room.

Strategy 25.   Get the participants engaged early in the meeting by using a visual starting question focused on key topics, personal outcomes, one-minute check-ins, or any other subject appropriate for the meeting.

Strategy 26.   Gain buy-in to the agenda by linking the participants' personal outcomes or key topics to the agenda.

Strategy 27.   Use ground rules to identify in-bounds and out-of-bounds behavior.

Strategy 28.   Establish parking boards to have a place to "park" decisions made, actions to be taken, or issues to be addressed at a later time.

Virtual Resource for You

The following resource is available on the Virtual Meetings Website to aid you in implementing the strategies in this chapter.

In our tools library, you will find the checklist for starting a meeting.
www.virtualmeetingsbook.com/tools

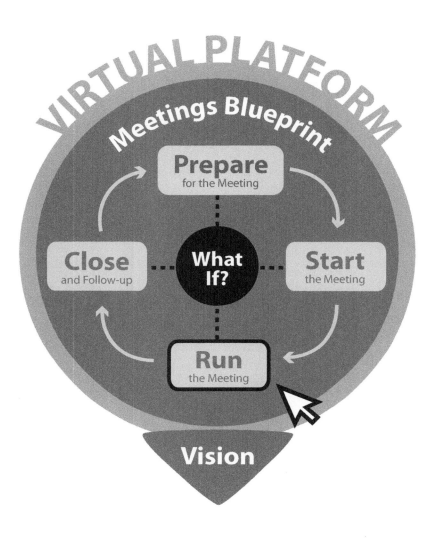

Running the Meeting | **6**

The Virtual Dilemma

You have successfully started the meeting for the performance review task force. You have covered the first agenda item by having the team outline how the current performance review process works. You are now ready to begin the process of defining problems and root causes. You know that some people won't necessarily understand the importance of doing this, and others will likely find the root cause analysis process a bit complicated— so you want to explain the purpose and give thorough directions without overdoing it and losing clarity. And depending on the virtual meeting platform you use, you won't necessarily be able to see people's body language and won't know whether they are really getting it.

In a virtual setting, how do you make sure you give directions that are concise, yet clear enough for people to understand?

Once you have gotten your virtual meeting started, you will run the meeting by executing the agenda and then close the meeting once all agenda items have been covered. The particular agenda item will dictate the specific steps you take while covering that item. As an overall framework for executing the meeting, however, consider using the following FIRST CLASS steps shown in Figure 6.1. See the "Virtual Resources for You" section at the end of this chapter to download a copy of the checklist for running a meeting.

This chapter covers all the FIRST CLASS steps that fall to the meeting leader, with the exception of dysfunctional behavior, disagreements, and closing the meeting—these three topics will be covered fully in subsequent chapters.

Figure 6.1: Checklist for Running a Meeting

Checklist for Running a Meeting (FIRST CLASS)

For each agenda item . . .

- ❑ **F**ocus the participants by providing an explanation of how the item furthers the meeting's purpose;

- ❑ **I**nstruct by providing clear and concise directions on how the agenda item will be executed;

- ❑ **R**ecord the appropriate information during the meeting;

- ❑ **S**eek consensus before moving on; and

- ❑ **T**rack time to ensure it is spent appropriately.

As needed . . .

- ❑ **C**ontrol and resolve any dysfunctional behavior quickly and effectively;

- ❑ **L**isten for off-topic discussions and redirect them to a parking board to keep the meeting focused;

- ❑ **A**ddress disagreements or conflicts that emerge;

- ❑ **S**eek all opinions and engage in a variety of ways; and

- ❑ **S**ummarize and close the meeting.

Focus the Participants (Checkpoint)

At the beginning of every agenda item, take a checkpoint to get everyone on the same page.[10]

Taking a Checkpoint

- Review: Quickly cover what has been done to date.
- Preview: Describe briefly what the group is about to do.
- Big View: Explain how the previewed agenda item fits into the meeting's overall purpose.

The checkpoint serves to ensure that all participants are aware that a transition is taking place. It also helps participants understand why the agenda item is being done and how it fits into the meeting's purpose. Finally, when you give a checkpoint at the beginning of every agenda item, the participants experience a smooth transition as you guide them through the meeting.

Sample Checkpoint

- We have just talked about how the performance review process works today. (Review)

- Our next step is to identify the problems and root causes of those problems. (Preview)

- This is important because if we identify the problems and root causes, we will be able to make sure that whatever solutions we create overcome these issues and result in a much better performance review process. (Big View)

Instruct through Clear Directions (PeDeQs)

After the checkpoint, you may ask your meeting participants to brainstorm, work in small teams, take a poll, etc. Depending on the activity, the quality of the directions that you provide can affect the success of that next step. As indicated in the virtual dilemma that started this chapter, a key for successful virtual meetings is the quality of the directions.

When giving directions, good meeting leaders describe what the participants are to do. However, great meeting leaders describe what to do, how to do it, and why doing it is important.

To ensure you cover the what, how, and why, consider giving directions by stepping through the PeDeQs.[11]

Providing Directions Using PeDeQs

- Give the overall **P**urpose of the activity.

- When appropriate, use a simple **E**xample that is outside the topic area.

- Give general **D**irections, using verbal pictures.

- Give specific **E**xceptions and special cases.

- Ask for **Q**uestions.

- Ask a **S**tarting Question that gets participants visualizing the answers.

As an example, suppose you want the participants in the meeting to identify the problems that occur in the organization's performance review process. Along with identifying the problems, you also want to identify the symptom and root causes for each of the problems. Figure 6.2 gives an example of the table to be completed, followed by an example of the PeDeQs dialogue.

Figure 6.2: Problem, Symptoms, Root Cause Table

Problem	Symptom	Root Cause

Sample PeDeQs Dialogue

- We will use this table to help identify the problems, symptoms, and root causes related to the performance review process. (Purpose)

- For example, if we wanted to drive our car, a problem might be a flat tire. The symptom might be that there is no air in the tire. The root cause might be that I haven't put air in the tire for a while. What else might be a root cause? (Example)

- Well, we're not driving a car. We are analyzing the problems with the performance review process. Here's how we will do it. First we will list all the problems. Then, once we have identified the problems, we will then determine a symptom and some root causes for each. (Directions)

- Now, there are a few other things you need to know. While we are discussing problems, you may come up with a root cause. I will place it in the root cause list until we identify the problem related to it. Likewise, after we list all the problems and are talking about symptoms and root causes, you may mention a problem, and I will add it to the bottom. (Exceptions)

- Any questions? (Questions)

- Okay, think about our last performance review cycle. Consider the things that were real problems, the things that frustrated you, and the things that worked very poorly or were just real problems. Think about the things that made you say, "There's got to be a better way to do this!" What are some of those frustrating problems with the current performance review process? (Starting question)

Record Relevant Information

After providing the directions and getting the process initiated, record—or have someone else record—the information provided by the participants. What should be recorded?

Items to Document in a Meeting

- **Decisions** made during the meeting
- **Actions** assigned during the meeting
- **Issues** that come up in the meeting to be discussed later

- **Relevant analysis and comments** covered during the meeting

We highly recommend using a virtual meeting platform that permits everyone to see the recorded comments, because of the following benefits.

Benefits of Having Participants See What is Recorded

- Keeps everyone on the same topic
- Discourages participants from repeating comments previously made
- Helps ensure that comments are recorded accurately
- Allows participants to easily and accurately refer to earlier comments
- Discourages multitasking by giving people a point of focus for the entire discussion

When recording information from the meeting, abide by the following recording rules to increase clarity and buy-in:

Recording Rules to Follow

Always record what was said before you respond.	$\Rightarrow$	Discourages you from recording only the points with which you agree
Record what they said, not what you heard.	$\Rightarrow$	Empowers the participants by ensuring that you use their words; helps prevent you from changing the words based on your bias

If it is appropriate, use a virtual meeting platform that permits the participants to record their own responses instead of your doing it. As described in Chapter 3, platforms that provide whiteboard-type features allow participants to contribute their own responses.

Seek Consensus before Moving On

Once you believe you have completed an agenda item, it is important to gain consensus before moving on. Gaining consensus prevents you, the meeting leader, from appearing to push a decision on participants before they are ready. How do you seek consensus?

Gaining Consensus to Move On

- Provide a brief summary of the information covered.
- Ask the participants, "Can we move on?"

The sample that follows provides a summary and then a check for consensus.

Sample Check for Consensus

- So, now we have identified twelve steps in the performance review process, including reviewing past accomplishments, rating performance areas, and identifying development needs. Are there other steps, or can we move on?

- Let's start with Ann and do a quick, alphabetical round-robin. Ann, are you ready to move on? Ben? Carla?

Track Time against the Agenda

As the meeting progresses, you should track time against your plan to ensure that the meeting time is spent in the most appropriate way.

Steps for Tracking Your Time

- Be sure to have a hard copy of a timed agenda that shows the amount of time to spend on each item.

- Note the end time for each agenda item and determine the amount of time ahead or behind schedule.

- Make adjustments in the target time for each following item as needed.

What should you do if the meeting falls behind? Strategies for addressing time issues will be covered later, in Part III.

Listen for Off-Topic Discussions

As participants interact during a meeting, you should monitor the discussion carefully to ensure that all comments are related to the agenda item under discussion. If the group begins to take a detour, you should bring the group back by asking a redirection question, as follows.

Sample Redirection Question

Meeting Leader:	What other steps are there in the performance review process?
Ann:	One of the things I think we really need to fix is the length of the process. It just takes too long for us to complete all the performance reviews.
Meeting Leader:	The length of the process certainly sounds like a problem we will want to address. Is it okay if we put it on the issues lists so we remember it when we talk about problems and then see if there are any other steps in the performance process we still need to list?
Ann:	Sure, go ahead. I just wanted to make sure we didn't miss this.

The traditional form of the redirection question is to affirm the value of the comment, ask permission to post it on the issues lists, and remind the group of the topic at hand: "That's an interesting point. Can we put that on the issues list so we don't forget it, and then get back to our question?"

When you use a redirection question, it is important to ask for permission to table the issue. By asking, you get the participant's buy-in. You may still get a verbal agreement if you just tell the participant that you are going to table the issue, but if that person quietly disagrees, you may be setting yourself up for a power struggle later.

What do you do if you ask for permission to table the issue and the participant disagrees? You put the question to the group (or to the meeting sponsor, if that is more appropriate).

Sample Redirection Question—Denied!

Meeting Leader:	The length of the process certainly sounds like a problem we will want to address. Is it okay if we put it on the issues lists so we remember it when we talk about problems and then see if there are any other steps in the hiring process we still need to list?
Ann:	No, I think this is something we should discuss now.
Meeting Leader:	That would be a detour off our main course, but if the group is for it, we can do it. How much time do you think we'll need, Ann?
Ann:	Only about ten minutes.
Meeting Leader:	Let's check in. Group, the plan has been to talk about the steps in the current process first and then the problems with the process. Ann would like to spend about ten minutes talking about the problem related to the length of the process and then we would get back to the discussion of the other steps. Ann, is that a clear description, or is there anything you would like to add?
Ann:	No, that's good.
Meeting Leader:	We typically go with a simple majority for these kinds of process decisions. Any other comments from anyone? . . . Okay then, let's do a round-robin to determine those in favor of taking ten minutes now to talk about the problem related to length of the process.

Seek All Opinions and Engage in a Variety of Ways

As indicated earlier, one of the fundamental issues with virtual meetings is keeping people fully engaged and participating as if they were in the same room. Therefore, we recommend having a meaningful, interactive activity that engages all participants every ten to twenty minutes.

Just as in face-to-face meetings, there are several ways to boost interactivity in a virtual meeting. We have listed several common engagement strategies in the list that follows, each of which is described in greater detail in Chapter 7.

Common Engagement Strategies for Virtual Calls

- Use round-robins frequently to gain everyone's input. For example, going back to our performance review process, you might introduce a round-robin as follows, "I would like to build a list of the strengths of the current performance review process. Let's go through the roll call list starting with Joe. Think about . . ."

- The whip is an engagement strategy that can be just as effective in virtual meetings as it is in face-to-face meetings. With the whip, the meeting leader asks a question and gives people a brief moment (thirty seconds or less) to think about a one-to-three word answer to the question. For example, "I would like to get the one word that best describes your opinion of the current performance review process? Think about . . ."

- Use polls, a feature of many virtual meeting platforms, to have group members indicate their preferences or beliefs. For example, you might have a poll such as this: "In general, what has been the average time it has taken to prepare an employee performance review? (A) Under one hour; (B) one to two hours; (C) two to three hours; or (D) over three hours?"

- Employ the whiteboard feature of the virtual meeting platform to brainstorm. For example, the whiteboard feature might be used to brainstorm the following question: "What are the problems with the performance management process?" The whiteboard allows many people to record answers at one time, making a round-robin unnecessary.

- Use breakout groups to have people work in teams. For example, you might have each breakout group take a separate performance review issue and identify potential solutions. Warning: Be aware that at the time of this edition, the "breakout rooms" feature of many virtual technology tools is not as reliable or user-friendly as other features. The splitting of audio and video between "rooms" and then pulling the information back may require a tech-savvy meeting leader. Be sure that you are not only competent in, but also comfortable with, the use of this feature.

Avoid Questions That Can't Be Answered by One Person

When asking questions, be very conscious of your wording to avoid silence. Avoid asking a question that no person in the group can answer individually. For example, instead of asking, "Is everyone okay with the agenda?" you might ask instead, "Would anyone like to recommend a change to the agenda?" If the group is small enough (twelve or fewer participants), use a roll call with direct questions such as, "Would anyone like to recommend a change to the agenda? Let's do a quick roll call with the question. Ann, any changes? Ben? Carla?"

Summary: The Strategies for Running a Virtual Meeting

In summary, the strategies for running virtual meetings effectively include the following:

Strategy 29. To get everyone on the same page and achieve a smooth flow through the agenda, take a checkpoint at the beginning of every agenda item.

- Review quickly what has been done to date.

- Describe briefly what the group is about to do.

- Explain how the previewed agenda item fits into the meeting's overall purpose.

Strategy 30. When giving directions, describe what to do, how to do it, and why doing it is important. Use the PeDeQs format.

- Give the overall **P**urpose of the activity.

- When appropriate, use a simple **E**xample that is outside the topic area.

- Give general **D**irections using verbal pictures.

- Give specific **E**xceptions and special cases.

- Ask for **Q**uestions.

- Ask a **S**tarting Question that gets participants visualizing the answers.

Strategy 31. Record all key information provided during the meeting, including all issues, decisions, actions, and relevant analysis for future reference. Be sure to record the information without personal bias.

Strategy 32. Use a virtual meeting platform that permits everyone to see the recorded comments. Where appropriate, have the participants record their own responses rather than your doing it for them.

Strategy 33. Before moving on to the next agenda item, summarize the information covered and use a round-robin to ask the participants, "Can we move on?"

Strategy 34. Track time against your plan to ensure that the meeting time is spent in the most appropriate way.

Strategy 35. If the group begins to detour, bring the group back by asking a redirection question, "That's an interesting point. Can we put that on the issues list so we don't forget it, and then get back to our question?"

Strategy 36. Seek all opinions and engage in a variety of ways, including round-robins, whips, polls, whiteboards, and breakout groups.

Virtual Resources for You

The following resources are available on the Virtual Meetings Website to aid you in implementing the strategies in this chapter.

In our tools library, you will find the following:

• Checklist for running a meeting

• An on-screen timer you can use to track time

www.virtualmeetingsbook.com/tools

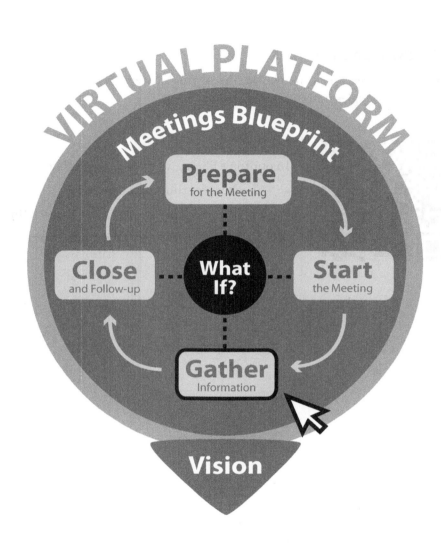

Gathering Information 7

- The Virtual Dilemma
- Brainstorming to Generate Ideas
- Feedback (Pro–Con Chart)
- Grouping to Categorize (Affinity Diagram)
- Listing to Gather Details
- Polling
- Prioritizing: The Check Method (Multi-voting)
- Question and Answer
- Round-Robin
- Small Group Breakout
- The Whip
- Summary: Strategies for Gathering Information
- Virtual Resource for You

The Virtual Dilemma

As the first meeting of the performance review improvement task force progresses, you begin to recognize that you are doing most of the talking. Each time you have paused and asked for questions, there has been a period of awkward silence, and no one speaks up. You are beginning to conclude that you should stop asking for questions and instead just assume that if people have questions, they will ask.

At the same time, however, you recognize that the lack of comments could mean that people aren't paying attention or that they simply aren't interested in the topic. You're not sure what to do.

Should you just assume there are no questions?
Or is there a way to ensure everyone is engaged?

As described in Chapter 1, engagement is critical for virtual meetings to gain the input and buy-in that yields better results. One way to ensure engagement is to use a variety of methods for gathering information from participants. For many agenda items in the typical virtual meeting, you will routinely use some way to gather information. These methods for getting information are most often called *information gathering processes*.[12]

Examples of Information Gathering Processes

- In a status meeting, a presentation-then-questions method is often used to gather information. A participant reports on the status; the leader and others in the meeting ask questions.

- In a meeting to generate ideas, a brainstorming method may be used in which participants provide as many ideas as possible before going back and analyzing each one.

- To put these ideas into categories, the participants may undertake a grouping process.

- To identify the top three items out of a list of twenty, a prioritizing process may be used.

- To evaluate the meeting's effectiveness, the leader may employ a feedback process.

Nearly every agenda item in a meeting uses some type of information gathering process. After all, if there were no need to gather any information, the meeting might as well be accomplished through an e-mail.

Unfortunately, most virtual meeting leaders do not plan the processes that they will use for each of the items in the agenda. As a result, during meetings, the most frequent processes used are "presentation-then-questions" and "brainstorming." But when you use the right process to address the specific need, and when you vary the way the processes are done, virtual meetings are more focused, more productive, and much more interesting for the participants. Figure 7.1 summarizes ten common information gathering processes used in virtual meetings and described in this chapter. See the "Virtual Resource for You" section at the end of this chapter to obtain additional engagement and information gathering strategies.

Figure 7.1: Ten Common Information Gathering Processes

Process	Purpose	Sample Use
Brainstorming	Generate ideas.	What could we do to address these problems?
Feedback	Collect opinions and input.	Let's take a minute to identify what went well in this meeting and what we need to improve.
Grouping	Categorize information.	Given these sixteen different problems, what are the three to five major categories they represent?
Listing	Create a list of details or known information.	What are the problems that occur in meetings?
Polling	Collect opinions.	Which of these statements best represents how you would like us to move forward?
Prioritizing	Identify items of greatest importance.	With twenty possibilities, which ones should be given priority?
Question & Answer	Identify and respond to specific questions.	What questions or issues do we have about this?
Round-robin	Gain input from all participants.	I would like to build a list of the strengths of the current process. Let's go through the roll call list starting with. . .
Small Group Breakout	Increase participation and efficiency.	Let's break into small groups and have each group develop answers for one of the issues.
The Whip	Gain rapid feedback.	Give a one or two-word response to the question, "How are you feeling about the session right now?"

Brainstorming to Generate Ideas

Purpose: Generate ideas

Sample Use: What could we do to improve our meetings?

1. Title your screen ahead of time.

2. Describe the activity and purpose; be sure to encourage creativity and out-of-the-ordinary ideas.

   "Our next step is to brainstorm potential improvements to our meetings. This is important because we don't want to continue to have bad meetings. Instead, we want to come up with solutions that can help us ensure that our meetings are effective, efficient, and productive."

3. Set a time limit and describe the general directions with an example if necessary; offer a response format, if appropriate.

   "We are going to take five minutes to do a round of intense brainstorming. I would like for us to go through the roll call list, starting with Joe, and have each person give me one thing we could do that would move us toward our vision of masterful virtual meetings. If you can, give me a 'verb–object' such as, 'Implement this. Develop that.'"

   "We will probably go around three or more times, so if you can't think of anything when it is your turn, just say 'pass.'"

4. Prohibit judgment of any type on an idea. If the idea does not meet the objective, record it anyway. Remind participants of the objective and keep moving.

   "Since we want to keep the creative juices flowing, it is important that during this phase we don't spend any time judging or analyzing the ideas. I will be typing as fast as I can, and we will be moving quickly from person to person. If you find yourself thinking, 'That won't work,' ask yourself, 'What will work? How can I improve on it?' Some of the best ideas start out as impractical suggestions."

5. Ask a starting question to help the group visualize their answers.

   "Let's go back to our list of problems and the categories. These are the things we have to fix. Think about things you've seen other companies do that you have thought we might do, and other things we could do to make our meetings much better. Joe, get me started. Let's build a list of some of the things we could do to improve our meetings. What are some of those things?"

6. Record responses.

7. Keep a steady pace. At this point, go for quantity rather than quality of ideas. The more ideas the better. Use a lot of fill-in words if necessary.

"Give me more. Who's next? More ideas, more ideas. . . . What other ways could we improve our meetings?"

8. End the brainstorming segment when the time limit is reached or when there is a round in which everyone passes. Ask for any last thoughts before closing.

   "We have reached our time limit. Any last-minute ideas to add?"

9. Always follow a brainstorming session with some type of grouping or prioritization activity to highlight the jewels.

10. Note that using a whiteboard in brainstorming allows everyone to type at once, which speeds the process.

The sample screen, Figure 7.2, represents information that could have been generated as a result of the brainstorming session described above:

Figure 7.2: Brainstorming Results

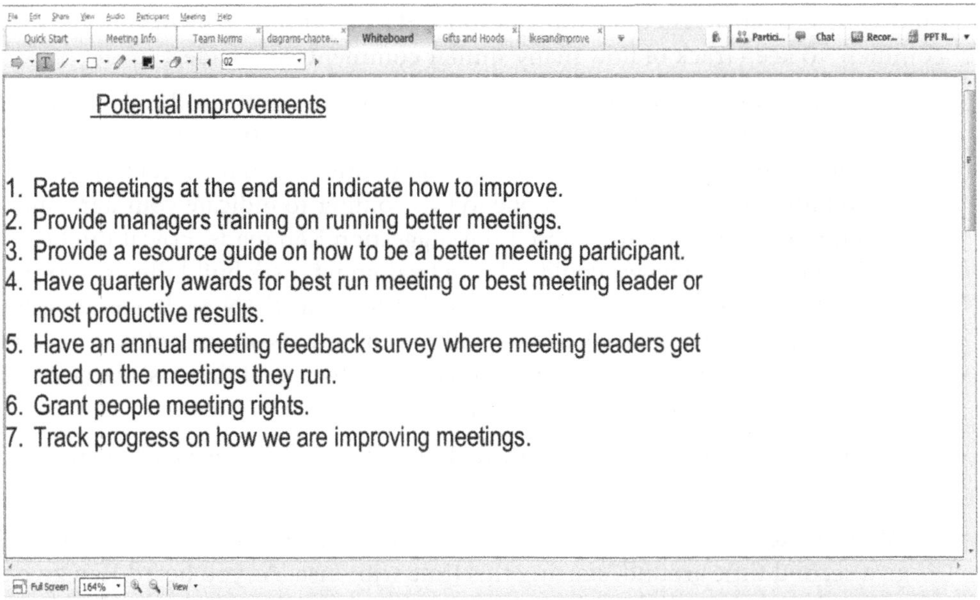

Potential Improvements

1. Rate meetings at the end and indicate how to improve.
2. Provide managers training on running better meetings.
3. Provide a resource guide on how to be a better meeting participant.
4. Have quarterly awards for best run meeting or best meeting leader or most productive results.
5. Have an annual meeting feedback survey where meeting leaders get rated on the meetings they run.
6. Grant people meeting rights.
7. Track progress on how we are improving meetings.

Feedback (Pro–Con Chart)

Purpose: Collect opinions and input

Sample Use: Let's take a minute to identify the strengths of and concerns about this suggestion.

Feedback is an important part of learning and improvement. Unfortunately, when the virtual meeting leader gives a suggestion, it is not unusual for everyone to say, "Yes, good idea," or when someone else gives an idea, it is not uncommon for the initial response to be, "No way, that won't work." While in the first case there might appear to be full agreement when there is not, in the second case, one person's initial negative comment can completely derail a potentially beneficial idea. Consider the following when seeking feedback on an idea or when evaluating an activity:

1. Title your screen ahead of time.

2. Describe the activity and purpose.

    "Ken has just shared his view on how we might address a manager who chronically has bad meetings. Let's get some input on this."

3. Provide the general directions.

    "Let's affirm Ken's contribution by quickly going around and saying what you like about the idea. Then we'll talk about concerns and ways to improve."

4. Start with strengths. Ask a starting question. Start a running tally next to the original comment to keep track of how many similar comments are made.

    "So, let's start with strengths. I would like to go through the roll call list, starting with Trina. I would like each one of you to identify one thing you liked about the suggestion. If someone has already said the thing you like, feel free to say, 'Ditto number two,' and I'll add one to this counter to indicate your agreement with the comment. So think about the suggestion Ken made, how it might work, and the benefits we could achieve by doing it. Let's build the list. Trina, get me started. What do you like about what Ken said?" (Note: In some cases, it will be appropriate to have just two or three comments on strengths instead of comments from the entire group. This is especially true if there is a large number of participants or if the suggestion is minor.)

5. Move on to concerns or ways to improve. Using the call list, have participants indicate suggestions.

    "We've talked about strengths. Let's move on to concerns or ways to improve. Let's go a second time around, starting this time with Lisa. As you heard Ken give the suggestion, you might have had concerns about it or thoughts on how to improve on it. Or if you don't, feel free to pass. Get me started, Lisa."

6. If appropriate, go back through the call list one last time and ask participants to indicate which improvement suggestions they support and indicate the number supporting each improvement by adding to the tally for each improvement suggestion.

    "Let's now go back through our call list one last time, starting with Joe, and indicate which improvement suggestions each participant agrees with by saying the number of the improvement. As you indicate your support, I will add to the tally so we can determine the overall level of support for each suggested improvement. Joe, get me started. Which improvement suggestions do you agree with?"

7. In some cases, having information on the number of people who support each improvement will be adequate. If full consensus is needed, you will use the consensus-building strategies described in Chapter 10.

Figure 7.3 provides a sample of results.

Figure 7.3: Feedback Results

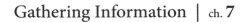

Strengths and Concerns	
Pace was good; just kept moving nicely	Would prefer a later start time (2)
Felt like a face-to-face meeting	Have someone from HR to review the SoP (1)
Engagement was good and varied	Rotate the meeting leadership so all learn how to run these virtually (5)
We got a lot done	
Started, and looks like we will end, on time	

Grouping to Categorize (Affinity Diagram)

Purpose: Categorize information

Sample Use: Given these twelve problems, what are the three to six major categories that they represent?

1. To prepare for grouping, title your screen ahead of time. Ensure the items to be grouped can be viewed on the screen for ease of reference. It may be appropriate to split your screen for this process, with one half the screen showing the list of items and the other half showing the names of the categories as you create them.

2. Describe the activity and purpose.

"Our next step is to take the items that we have created and group them into categories. We might end up with anywhere from three to six categories. By doing this, we will be better able to develop solutions for the category instead of solutions for the individual problems."

3.   Give the general directions.

"We will again use the call list starting with Trina, and I will step through the items one by one and ask one of you to name the category that the item should go in. If the category doesn't already exist, we will create a new one. At the end, we will review the categories by doing a final round-robin to make sure we are all comfortable."

4.   Read the first item and ask the participant you named to define the category for it. You might suggest a category for the first item to get the participants started.

"The first item says, 'No agenda.' Let's name the category in which 'no agenda' would be included. Trina, what would the category name be?"

"It sounds like this first one has to do with preparation; does that sound like a reasonable category, Trina?"

5.   Record the category name on a screen and label it "A." Place an "A" next to the first item in the brainstorm list to indicate which group it was put in. You may want to put the "A" in a font color different from the color used to create the original list so that the category label stands out.

6.   Go to the next item on the original list. Ask the next participant on the call list to determine whether it belongs in an existing group or whether a separate group is needed.

"The second item is 'minimal participation.' Should we group this with preparation or should it go in a different category, Lisa?"

7.   If the item belongs in an existing group, label the item with the category letter. If the item belongs in a new group, ask the participant for the name of the category, give the category a letter, and record the letter next to the item.

8.   Continue Steps 6 and 7 until all items on the original list have been categorized.

9.   Review the groups to determine if additional consolidation or category splitting is appropriate.

"Let's review what we have done to make sure the groups make sense. At this point, we have three items in each of our four categories. To ensure these seem appropriate, I will use our roll call list for a final round-robin starting with Lisa. Lisa do you see the need for any additional consolidation or category splitting?" (Continue through the roll call list.)

Figure 7.4 provides a sample of output from the grouping exercise described.

Figure 7.4: Grouping Results

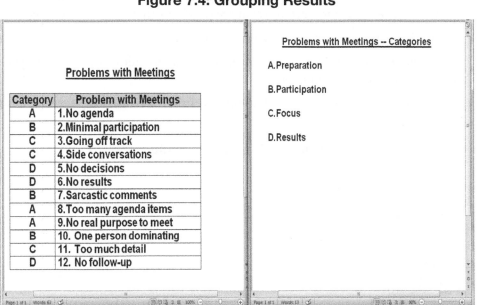

Listing to Gather Details

Purpose: Create a list of details or known information

Sample Use: What are common problems that occur in meetings?

1. Title your screen ahead of time.

2. Describe the activity and purpose.

   "Our next step is to identify common problems that occur in meetings. This step is important because by identifying the frequent problems that occur in our meetings, we will be able to develop a plan for addressing our specific problems."

3. Give general directions with an example if necessary.

   "I would like for us to go through the roll call list, starting with Pat, and have all of us identify one problem we have had in meetings. After we have gone around once, we'll come back and ask if anyone has other problems that haven't already been said. If it is your turn and you can't think of a different problem, just say, 'Pass.' Any questions?"

4. Ask a starting question to help the group visualize their answers.

   "Think about a meeting that you attended in the last sixty days that was a really bad meeting. Think about the things that didn't go well, the difficulties in the meeting, the problems that occurred, the things that happened that made the meeting not nearly as effective as it could have been. Let's build a list of those problems. Pat, get me started. What are problems that occur in meetings?"

5. Record the responses you receive from the participants.

6. Note that, just as in brainstorming, using a whiteboard allows everyone to type at once, which speeds the process.

Figure 7.5 provides a sample of a screen that might result from the listing exercise described.

Figure 7.5: Listing Results

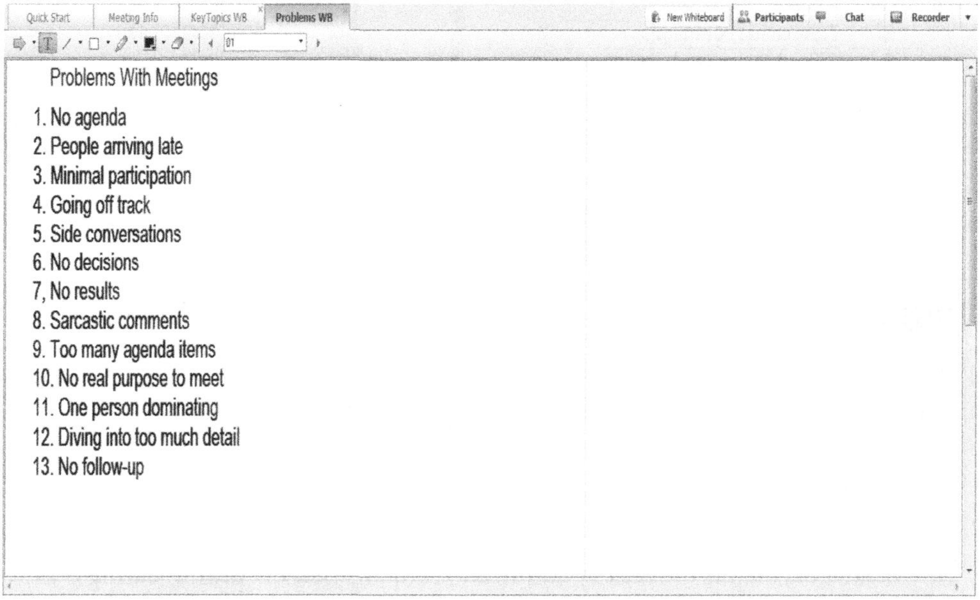

Polling

Purpose: Create the ability to gain feedback from meeting participants by selecting choices from a list of multiple items

Sample Use: Which of these statements best represents how you would like us to move forward?

1. Create your poll in advance or on the fly during a virtual meeting.

2. Describe the activity and purpose.

"Our next step is to identify how we would like to move forward in our work process. This step is important because we want to make sure we make the best use of everyone's time and not do any unnecessary activities."

3. Give the general directions with an example if necessary.

"In just a moment I am going to open up a poll. In this poll you will find the three alternatives that we identified in our last meeting. You will have thirty seconds to make your selection. Before I ask you to select, let me pause and ask if there are any questions?" Typically allow several seconds for participants to identify themselves by either "raising their hand" on the software, or identifying themselves to ask their question.

4. Ask a starting question to help the group visualize their answers.

"Think about the three alternatives that we identified in our last meeting. Think about the benefits of going in each of these directions, the results we would likely achieve. Think about the one you feel most confident will help us achieve our objective. Which is it? Please make that selection now."

5. Open the poll for voting. Announce as the participants respond the percentage that have responded and count down the time; close the poll when all participants have responded, or after about thirty seconds.

6. Share and announce the results of the poll.

"As you can see from the results of the poll the top choice is B. Any comments before we move forward with B?"

7. Note that in some cases you may want to use a consensus building strategy (e.g., informed majority described in Chapter 10) to give participants a forum for discussing the alternatives before taking the poll.

Figure 7.6 provides an example of results from a poll.

Figure 7.6: Polling Results

1. Which growth alternative would you prefer for our focus?	Results
a. Alternative #1: Expand by focusing on new product offerings in the existing customer base.	1/10 (10%)
b. Alternative #2: Expand by focusing on new vertical markets with existing products.	7/10 (70%)
c. Alternative #3: Expand by focusing on opening our initial international office.	2/10 (20%)

Prioritizing: The Check Method (Multi-voting)

Purpose: Identify items of greatest importance

Sample Use: With fifteen possibilities, which items should be given priority?

In face-to-face meetings, there are a number of methods to prioritizing, including raising hands, secret ballots, using dots, and weighted scoring. In a virtual meeting, we find the preferred approach is the check method using an annotation feature in the virtual meeting platform. We describe the check method below.

1. Prepare your screen ahead of time.

2. Describe the activity and purpose.

    "Our next step is to prioritize these improvements in order to identify the ones that we should begin implementing first."

3. Give general directions.

    "We will start by identifying the most important criteria to use in our prioritization. I will then give each person a specific number of checks they may use to indicate those improvements that they feel will have the greatest effect on our meetings. The improvements with the most checks will be the ones that we will consider for initial implementation."

    "Before we start voting with our checks, however, we will have a special lobbying period. See, if I were participating in the voting, I would want everyone to vote the way I would vote. I would hate it if the improvement I believed was the most important received only my vote. The lobbying period is intended to address this.

Before anyone votes with their checks, each of us will have one minute to share with the whole group what we believe are the key items to get votes and, most importantly, why. We will start the lobbying using our roll call list and begin with Ken. After everyone who wants to has taken their sixty seconds to lobby, we will then vote using our checks."

"So to recap: First, we will talk about the criteria to use in selecting our priorities; second, we will have a lobbying period; and finally, we will vote and review the outcome. Any questions?"

4. Suggest criteria to the team and ask for others before seeking acceptance.

"There are three criteria (type the criteria on the screen for visibility) that we typically like to keep in mind when prioritizing. The level of impact is perhaps most important: What will be the impact of this improvement on the overall performance review process? High, medium, or low? Probability of success is our second criterion. If we choose to implement this improvement, how likely is it that we will succeed given the nature of the improvement, our skill sets, and other factors? Finally, we look at cost-effectiveness. How cost-effective is this improvement compared to others in terms of providing the biggest bang for the buck? Let's use our roll call list, starting with Lisa to determine if there are other criteria to add. Lisa, are there other criteria you suggest we keep in mind?"

5. After establishing the criteria, provide an opportunity for each person to lobby the group for support.

"We have determined the criteria. Now, before we vote with our checks, we will all have the option of taking one minute to indicate those improvements we think should be given highest priority and explain why. The 'why' is the most important part because it will give each of us a better understanding of the value of the improvement. I would like to use our call list starting with Tony and go through the roll call list. Each person can 'pass or play.' Tony, what do you think? Would you like to pass or lobby the group?"

6. Establish the total number of checks each participant will use. The number of checks should equal twenty to thirty percent of the total number of items. For example, if there are twenty items, consider giving each person four to six checks. To get a wider range of priority scores, consider using both a check mark and an X-mark worth different values.

"Now that lobbying is complete, let's determine our priorities. You have been given three green check marks and two red X-marks. Each green check mark counts three points and each red X-mark counts one point. Place the green checks on the three improvements that you believe are the most important. Place the red X-marks on two other improvements that you would like to see happen as well. You cannot place more than one mark on an item."

"You will have five minutes to place your votes. As you are voting, keep in mind the criteria we decided. Any questions?"

7. Review the results and ask for consensus to move forward with the voted priorities. If you do not have consensus, use consensus-building strategies described in Chapter 10 to resolve the issue.

"Of the fifteen improvements resulting from the brainstorming activity, it appears that only seven received any votes at all. Of the seven, the top five vote-getters are clearly the winners."

"While we may be able to implement all of these, it is clear that the ones to start with are the following. . . . Let's go through the roll call list, starting with Joe, and check for consensus. Give me a 'yea' if you're okay with these priorities or a 'nay' if you have an issue with them. Joe, get us started. Are you a yea or a nay with starting with these five?"

Figure 7.7 represents information that could have been generated as a result of the prioritization session described above.

Figure 7.7: Prioritization Results

Priority of Improvements

Tally	Priorities
3333331 (19)	1. Rate meetings at the end and indicate how to improve.
3333311 (17)	2. Provide managers training on running better meetings.
33331 (13)	3. Provide a resource guide on how to be a better meeting participant.
31111 (7)	4. Have quarterly awards for best run meeting or best meeting leader or most productive results.
1 (1)	5. Have an annual meeting feedback survey where meeting leaders get rated by their people.
33111 (9)	6. Grant people meeting rights.
1 (1)	7. Track progress on how we are improving meetings.

Note: ("3" represents the check marks, which count for three points each; "1" represents the x-marks, which count for one point each. The total score is shown in italics in parentheses.)

Question and Answer

Purpose: Identify and respond to specific questions

Sample Use: What questions or issues do we have about this?

To maximize the question-and-answer period, consider gathering all questions at once, grouping the questions, and then having the answerer respond to a group of questions all at the same time. This approach helps to ensure that the most critical questions get answered first, and it provides a full view of all questions so that the time spent responding can be better managed.

1. Title your screen ahead of time.

2. Describe the activity and purpose.

    "Now that we have heard an expert speak on transforming meetings inside our organization, let's take a minute to identify the additional questions we want answered. This will allow us to get all the questions at once and will give our speaker a chance to cover all the questions."

3. Give directions to the participants, including where on the call list you will begin and how many rounds you will use to gather their questions as you record their questions on the screen.

    "We will use our roll call list, starting with Andrea, and ask each of you to identify the most important question that you would like to see answered as a result of this presentation. Please provide your question or indicate pass when it is your turn. We will use three round-robins or until there is a round with no new questions. Any questions?"

4. Ask a starting question to help the group visualize their answers.

    "We just heard a presentation on strategies used by other organizations to improve meetings. Think about the things you heard, the things you want to hear more about, and the specific questions that will help us design our own meetings transformation process. Andrea, get us started. What is a question you would like to see answered? . . . Bob, you are next. . . ."

5. Review the questions and then use the grouping technique to create categories for them.

    "It looks like we have a total of fifteen questions. We will use our roll call list, starting with Tony, to group our questions into categories. This will allow us to address all related questions at one time. The first question reads, 'Has any organization you know of actually granted their employees meeting rights?' Tony, what would be an appropriate name for the first category? Okay, so we have

Category A—Empowering. Bob, what about the second question? It says . . . Does this go with the Empowering category or does it need a new category? Okay, let's go to the next question . . ."

6. Do a checkpoint and turn it over to the speaker to respond to the questions.

"We have identified the key questions we want to have answered and grouped them into five categories. Now let's turn it over to the speaker who will use our last thirty minutes to cover each group of questions. This will help ensure that we get to the most important questions. And if time remains, we will open it up to the floor for additional questions. So, let's hear from our speaker who will tell us which group of questions to tackle first . . ."

Figure 7.8 provides results from a Q-and-A grouping.

Figure 7.8: Question-and-Answer Groupings

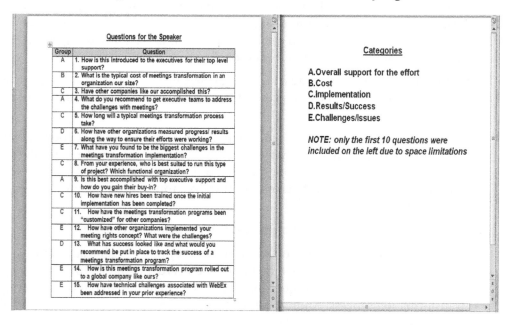

Round-Robin

Purpose: Gain input from all participants

Sample Use: I would like to build a list of the strengths of the current
               process. Let's go through the roll call list starting with . . .

The round-robin technique is usually coupled with another engagement strategy (e.g., brainstorming, listing, polling, prioritizing) to ensure your gain input from all participants.

1. Start by stating your purpose.

   > "I would like to build a list of the strengths of the current performance review process."

2. Announce who will be going first. Doing this makes it more likely that the person will hear the question when you ask it and be ready with an answer.

   > "Let's go through the roll call list starting with Joe."

3. Ask your starting question based on the engagement strategy you will be using as part of the round-robin.

   > "Think about the last performance review cycle. Think about the things you liked about it, the things that went well, and the things that really worked. Let's build a list of those things. Joe, get us started. What is a strength of our current performance review process?"

4. With round-robins, you should vary the starting point so that the same person isn't always going first.

5. Regardless of the starting point, be sure to follow the same order each time, calling people by name. This allows people to prepare an answer and the meeting to flow quickly. Establish this order early in the meeting.

6. Use round-robins frequently to gain everyone's input.

Small Group Breakout

Purpose: Increase participation, efficiency, group energy, and focus

Sample Use: Can we break into small groups and have each group develop answers for one of the problem categories?

Breakout groups are especially appropriate when the agenda calls for a process to be performed several times (for example, to identify solutions to the four categories of meeting problems).

1. Let the participants know that they are about to break out.

   > "In a minute we will be breaking out into groups to identify up to three priority strategies for addressing each of our categories of problems with meetings."

2. Complete the first element with the entire group.

   > "Before we break out into groups, however, I would like for us to tackle one of the

categories together so that everyone is aware of what we are trying to do, how to do it, and what the products looks like that each team will create."

"Let's work together on . . . We will first spend five minutes brainstorming solutions. We will then have a lobbying period to discuss the solutions each of us believes have the greatest potential. Then we will vote to select our top three. Let's start by . . ."

3. Divide into teams.

"We have three additional categories of problems, so let's break into three teams by counting off by threes. . . . If you would now, let's have all the ones over here, all the twos over there using our virtual meeting platform's breakout feature . . ."

4. Appoint team leaders and scribes/reporters.

"We need to appoint team leaders. I would like the person on your team whose first name is closest to the end of the alphabet serve as the team leader in each breakout group. The person whose name is next closest to the end alphabetically will serve as the scribe and the reporter for the breakout."

5. Give final directions to the teams covering the timeframe, product, process for creating it, and a progress milestone (e.g., how far you should be when half the time has passed), and then start the breakout rooms.

"Before you start, let me review the instructions. You will have thirty minutes to identify up to three top strategies for addressing the category of meeting problems assigned to your team. The process is to first spend five minutes on brainstorming solutions. You will then have a lobbying period to discuss the solutions that each team member believes have the greatest potential. Then you will vote to select up to three. As a milestone for you, by the end of twenty minutes, you should have started the lobbying period. Any questions?"

6. Monitor the activity.

As the virtual breakout teams are working, you will want to move from breakout room to breakout room to monitor the activity. Specifically, you will want to ensure that each team is progressing as expected, that the deliverable items are reasonably close to what is desired, and that the timeframe is being met.

7. Close the breakout rooms and have each team report their results.

"Now that we are done, let's hear from each team. You will have three minutes to describe the solutions that your team developed and to explain why these are most appropriate."

The Whip

Purpose: Gain rapid feedback by having everyone respond with a very short answer to a question

Sample Use: Give a one- or two-word response to the question, "How are you feeling about the session right now?"

1. Describe the purpose clearly.

    "We are about halfway through our agenda for the meeting, and I would like to take a temperature check to determine how people are feeling about the session."

2. Provide instructions.

    "Let's do a round-robin starting with Rick, and we will go down the roll call list from there. I am looking for everyone to give a one- or two-word response to the question, 'How are you feeling about the session right now?'"

3. Make sure everyone is ready.

    "Before we start, I want to make sure we all have our one or two words ready because once we start, it will go very fast. So, I am starting with Rick and asking first if you are ready. Say yes if you have your one- or two-word answer to the question, 'How you are feeling about the session right now?'"

4. Get started.

    "Okay, it sounds like everyone is ready. So, let's get started with Rick, and we will go quickly down the roll call list. Rick, get me started. What is your one or two-word response to the question, 'How are you feeling about the session right now?'"

5. Reflect on what was heard.

    "Let's reflect now on what we just heard. Given the comments, are there changes anyone would like to suggest regarding how we spend the second half of the meeting?"

6. While you will be getting all views, it may be helpful to the group to start with someone who will readily have a response and who tends to be fairly positive in his/her reactions. This will get the session off to a positive start.

7. There is no need to record the comments from the whip, as it will slow down the group.

8. It may be important for the group to make a decision based on the suggestions that come from the reflection on what was heard. If so, consider using the informed majority (Chapter 10) process for this purpose.

Summary: Strategies for Gathering Information

In summary, strategies for gathering information effectively in masterful virtual meetings include the following:

Strategy 37.   For each agenda item in the virtual meeting, use the appropriate process based on the purpose of the agenda item.

Strategy 38.   To generate ideas, use brainstorming.

Strategy 39.   To create a list of details, use listing.

Strategy 40.   To categorize information, use grouping.

Strategy 41.   To identify items of most importance, use prioritizing.

Strategy 42.   To collect opinions and input, use feedback or polling.

Strategy 43.   To gain rapid feedback, use the whip.

Strategy 44.   To increase participation and efficiency, use breakouts.

Strategy 45.   To identify and respond to specific questions, use Q-and-A.

Strategy 46.   To gain a response from everyone, use a round-robin.

Virtual Resource for You

The following resource is available on the Virtual Meetings Website to aid you in implementing the strategies in this chapter.

In our tools library, you will find additional engagement strategies for your use in keeping participants engaged and interacting.

www.virtualmeetingsbook.com/tools

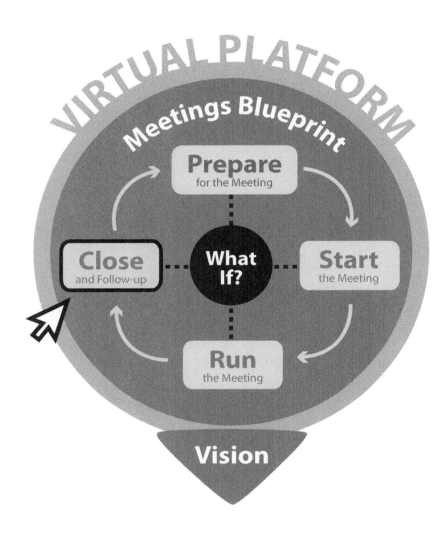

Closing and Follow-up | 8

- The Virtual Dilemma
- Checklist for Closing and Follow-up
- Review Items Covered in the Meeting
- Confirm Decisions Made
- Address Outstanding Issues
- Assign Actions
- Evaluate the Meeting
- Thank Participants and End the Meeting
- Document and Distribute Meeting Notes
- Follow Up to Hold People Accountable
- Summary: The Strategies for Closing and Follow-up
- Virtual Resources for You

The Virtual Dilemma

You have reached the end of the agenda and are ready to wrap up the meeting. The team has made two decisions that appear on the decisions list. There also are two actions on the action lists and three items on the issues list. While it is clear to you what will happen with the decisions and the actions, you are not sure what should be done about the open issues. Should you just ignore them and assume that if they are important, they will come up again? Or should you bring them up to the team before closing and risk that the meeting will be extended?

At the end of the meeting, what should you do with open issues?

Once all agenda items have been covered, it is time to close the meeting. Before closing, there are a number of items to be covered, and after closing, follow-up is often needed. This chapter covers both closing and following up as shown in Figure 8.1.

Figure 8.1: Checklist for Closing and Follow-up

Checklist for Closing and Follow-up

❑ Review the items covered in the meeting.
❑ Confirm the decisions made.*
❑ Address outstanding issues.*
❑ Ensure that all actions have names and dates assigned.*
❑ Evaluate the meeting.
❑ Thank participants and end the meeting.*
❑ Document and distribute meeting notes.
❑ Follow up to hold people accountable for assigned actions.*

* = Recommended for all meetings

As with prior chapters on preparing and starting, not all meetings will require all the closing and follow-up steps. The closing can take as little as five minutes and as long as forty-five minutes, or even longer depending on the size of the group and the steps you use. You should adjust the list as appropriate for the meetings you lead. Those items asterisked (*) should be done for every meeting, regardless of the number of participants. See the "Virtual Resources for You" section at the end of this chapter to download a copy of the closing checklist.

Review Items Covered in the Meeting

Before ending the meeting, go back to the agenda and summarize all the activities completed during the meeting.

- The review provides the participants with a reminder of what was done. It also can provide a sense of accomplishment.

    "Let's step through the agenda and identify what has been accomplished during this meeting."

- If key topics or participant outcomes were identified, review each one to ensure coverage.

    "Let's also ensure that each key topic was covered or if we need to add any of these to the agenda for our next meeting."

Confirm Decisions Made

Next, review the decisions list, the parking board used to record decisions.

- The goal of the decision review is to **remind the team of the decisions** that have been made.

    "Let's next review the decisions we made during this meeting. I will walk through each one. Stop me if any one of them is not recorded correctly."

- Following the meeting, participants may be asked why specific decisions were made. To prepare participants for the discussion, consider taking time in the closing to **document the benefits of each decision**.

    "To help ensure that we all understand why each decision was made, let's take a moment to add one or two bullet points to each decision to document the benefit we expect to gain. Let's start with this first one, which says . . . Think about the benefits to be gained from this. Let's list one or two of these."

Address Outstanding Issues

The issues lists was the place that you parked topics that arose during the meeting that either needed to be covered at a later time or were completely irrelevant to the meeting. At the end of the meeting, it is important to clear all remaining items off this list.

Questions to Ask to Clear the Issues List

As a systematic way to quickly process the issues list, ask these questions in the following order for each issue:

- "Have we covered it?" (If so, move on to the next issue.)
- "Do we need to cover it?" (If not, move on to the next issue.)
- "Do we need to cover it now?"
    - Yes: Set a time limit and lead the discussion.
    - No: Move the issue to the action lists.

Assign Actions

The actions list contains activities to be performed sometime after the completion of the meeting and includes three columns, as shown in Figure 8.2.

Figure 8.2: The Action lists

Action	Who	When
1.		
2.		
3.		

Questions to Ask about Actions

- "Does this action still need to be accomplished?" (If not, discard it and move on to the next action.)
- "Who should do it?"
    - It is not appropriate to assign an action to someone not in the room.
    - If the action is best performed by someone outside the room, assign it to a person of authority in the room who will then ask the other person to perform the action.
- "By what date will you have it completed?"
    - If appropriate, let the person responsible for the action set the date for completion.

Evaluate the Meeting

Feedback from meeting participants can provide valuable insights on how to continuously improve virtual meetings. Consider combining the feedback steps described in Chapter 7 with a brief rating system.

1. Start with strengths.

    "Let's start with strengths. I would like to go through the roll call list, starting with Andrea. I would like all of us to identify one thing we liked about the meeting and the way we worked. If someone has already said the thing you like, feel free to say, 'Ditto number one.'"

    "So, think about the things you liked about the meeting, the things that went well, the times that people seemed to be engaged, and the things that really worked. Let's build the list. Andrea, get me started. What did you like about the meeting? What went well?"

2. Rate the meeting.

    "Let's rate the meeting on our key criteria. Remember our rating system: 3 means the meeting was well done, 2 means it was adequate, and 1 means it was insufficient. How would you rate . . ."

    The preparation and start? (e.g., the meeting notice, participants prepared, on-time start, and clear purpose and agenda)

    Staying focused? (e.g., keeping on track and appropriate detail)

    Group dynamics? (e.g., working together, everyone engaged, handling disagreements, and minimizing dysfunction)

    The results? (e.g., good decisions, clear actions, and follow-up plan)

    Overall rating?

3. Move on to ways to improve.

    "We've talked about strengths and rated the meeting. Let's move on to ways to improve. Let's go around a second time, starting this time with Sandy. Take a look at the ratings, especially the lower ones. Think about the things that could have happened that would have improved these ratings: things we should consider doing differently next time. What would you suggest that we do differently that would have made the meeting even better? Get me started, Sandy."

4. Review each improvement suggestion and ask to determine the number of people in support of each.

    "Let's go back now over each improvement suggestion. I would like to get a rough indication of the level of support for each one. As I read each suggestion, click on the 'raise your hand' button if you agree with that suggestion. The first says . . .

How many people agree that this suggestion would have improved the meeting? That looks like about eighty percent. Click off your raised hand button and let's move on to the next . . ."

Thank Participants and End the Meeting

Finally, end the meeting by expressing to the participants your appreciation for their attendance, reminding them of the next steps, and adjourning the meeting.

- "Thank you for participating in this meeting."
- "You should be receiving documentation of this meeting within seven days."
- "Our next meeting is on [date] at [time] in this same virtual meeting room. I look forward to interacting with you all then."
- "This meeting is officially adjourned!"

Document and Distribute Meeting Notes

What should be documented and included in the meeting notes? Consider the following.

Items to Document in Meeting Notes

- **Decisions** made during the meeting*
- **Actions** assigned during the meeting*
- **Issues** that come up in the meeting to be discussed later, if any
- **Relevant analysis and comments** covered during the meeting

While not all items are required in the documentation that follows every meeting, the asterisked (*) items should always be documented. The final documentation will also include notes added by the documenter to provide clarity or build context for the reader. Consider italicizing notes added by the documenter to differentiate these notes from information provided by the participants. Figure 8.3 gives an example of meeting notes. See the "Virtual Resources for You" section at the end of this chapter to download a meeting notes template.

Figure 8.3: Sample Meeting Notes

The Meetings Transformation Team
Meeting Notes from xx/xx/xx

The Meetings Transformation Team held its first meeting on xx/xx/xx from 9:00 a.m. to 11:00 a.m., ET. The meeting was virtual. Attendees of the meeting were the following people:

- ☐ Kathy K., team leader
- ☐ Cleve C., documenter
- ☐ Ken M.
- ☐ Bill G.
- ☐ Vanessa R
- ☐ Trina J.
- ☐ Andrea T.

The following are the meeting notes from the meeting. *Items appearing in italics indicate information added by the documenter for clarity or to provide context.*

A. Meeting Purpose and Agenda

Following the welcome, the team leader presented and gained agreement on the following purpose and agenda for the meeting.

Meeting Purpose

To confirm the project objective and gain agreement on the work process and our operating norms.

Meeting Agenda

A. Welcome, purpose, and agenda
B. Review the team's objective
C. Identify critical issues for accomplishing the team's objective
D. Review the team's work process (*the Master Plan*)
E. Define team norms and decision-making method
F. Decide logistics for meetings
G. Begin team work process (if time permits)
H. Define next steps

B. Team Objective

The team leader provided team members with copies of the team's objective below, which was crafted by the organization's leadership team.

The overall objective of the Meetings Transformation Team is to help make our meetings more effective, more efficient, and more productive.

C. Critical Issues

Team members were asked to identify the key items that they felt needed to be addressed in order to ensure we achieved our objective. These items are listed below. The team leader indicated that, throughout the process, we will be coming back to this list and adding to it to ensure that all issues are covered.

- Getting everyone on board
- Addressing managers who chronically lead bad meetings
- Avoiding starting with a bang and then fizzling out
- Determining how to measure our success
- How to participate on this team while maintaining full work responsibilities
- Identifying when we are done

D. The Master Plan

The team leader presented the Master Plan—a proposed work process. After a lengthy discussion, the team agreed to the following work tasks:

- Identify the problems we see in our meetings to provide a starting list of what needs to be fixed.
- Conduct a meeting survey to document a baseline of how we are performing with meetings.
- Finalize your meeting rights, our meeting vision, and our master plan.
- Finalize measurable outcomes that will define success for the initiative.
- Develop a support plan—including training, tutorials, and samples—to build up skills in those who lead or participate in meetings.
- Develop our plan for rewards and accountability.
- Develop our plan for monitoring progress and communicating results.
- Present a draft to senior management for approval.
- Refine recommendations based on senior management input.
- Execute the Master Plan, including monitoring results.

E. Define Team Norms and Decision-Making Method

The participants agreed to the following norms for the team:

- We will fully participate in each meeting.
- We will have one conversation at a time.
- We will leave cell phones off.
- We will speak positively of the team and of each other.
- We will respect one another's time by arriving at least five minutes in advance for all meetings so that we can start on time.
- We will take personal responsibility to be prepared for each meeting by reading all materials in advance.
- We will speak up about any issues or concerns we have.
- We will use five-finger consensus for all major decisions.

F. Decide Logistics for Meetings

The participants agreed to the following parameters for our meeting:

- We will meet every other Thursday from 1:00 p.m. to 3:00 p.m. ET.

G. What Are Existing Problems with Meetings?

The team began its work process by identifying existing problems with meetings.

- No agenda
- People arriving late
- Minimal participation
- Going off track
- Side conversations
- No decisions
- No results
- Sarcastic comments
- Too many agenda items
- No real purpose to meet
- One person dominating
- Diving into too much detail
- No follow-through

H. Next Steps

The team will meet again on zz/zz/zz from 1:00 p.m. to 3:00 p.m. ET. Our focus will be on the following:

- Review action lists.
- Define Step 2: Meeting Survey.
- Define Step 3: Meeting Vision Components.
- Discuss how to participate on the team and still get a full workload done (this may entail a recommendation to the leadership team).

I. Decisions List

The following is an ongoing list of decisions made by the team with the date when the decision was made.

1. We agreed to team norms (xx/xx/xx).
2. We agreed on our work process (xx/xx/xx).
3. We will meet every other Thursday, 1:00- 3:00 p.m. ET (xx/xx/xx).

J. Actions List

The following is an ongoing list of actions to be taken outside of the meeting along with the due date and the person responsible. When an action is completed, it appears in the next meeting notes as "done" and is then removed from subsequent meeting notes.

1. Document and distribute the meeting notes. (Bill G., nn/nn/nn)
2. Review the draft survey and the draft meeting vision components from the book, and come to the meeting with recommended changes. (All, zz/zz/zz)

Follow Up to Hold People Accountable

To ensure that actions assigned during the meeting are accomplished, consider follow-up actions such as the following.

Strategies to Encourage Follow-Through on Actions

- In the body of the e-mail that accompanies the meeting notes, remind the participants that actions are included that need to be completed prior to the next meeting.

- Several days before the next meeting, distribute an e-mail that highlights the actions to be completed prior to the next meeting.

- On the agenda for the next meeting, include a review of prior actions as the first or second agenda item.

- At the next meeting, ask people to report on those actions due to be completed.

  - Applaud those items completed on time.

  - For those items not completed, ask the person responsible to provide a revised deadline.

If follow-through appears to be a problem, consider having the team agree on a consequence list (e.g., twenty push-ups, sending everyone a gift certificate for lunch, providing the minutes for the next three meetings) when an assigned date for an action is missed more than once.

Summary: The Strategies for Closing and Follow-up

In summary, the strategies for closing virtual meetings and following up effectively include the following:

Strategy 47.   Before closing the meeting, thoroughly review the following:

- The agenda and all items covered in the meeting and any key topics or participant outcomes identified at the start

- The decisions made by the team, documenting benefits if necessary

- Any open issues in order to determine what action, if any, is needed on them

- All actions to ensure that a person and a date are assigned to each

Strategy 48.   Use a brief process of identifying strengths, improvements, and a rating for the meeting to gain valuable feedback on how to improve future meetings.

Strategy 49.   To maintain clarity around decisions made and actions to be taken as a result of the meeting, distribute a summary following the meeting that includes decisions, actions, open issues, and relevant analysis documented during the meeting.

Strategy 50.   To help ensure that actions assigned during the meeting are accomplished, distribute a notice highlighting actions to be completed several days before the next meeting. Additionally, in the next meeting, include a review of prior actions as the first or second agenda item.

Virtual Resources for You

The following resources are available on the Virtual Meetings Website to aid you in implementing the strategies in this chapter.

In our tools library, you will find the following:

- Checklist for closing a meeting

- A template for meeting notes

www.virtualmeetingsbook.com/tools

- Chapter 9.   What If There Is Dysfunction?
- Chapter 10. What If There Is Disagreement?
- Chapter 11. What If the Meeting Is a Special Virtual Case?

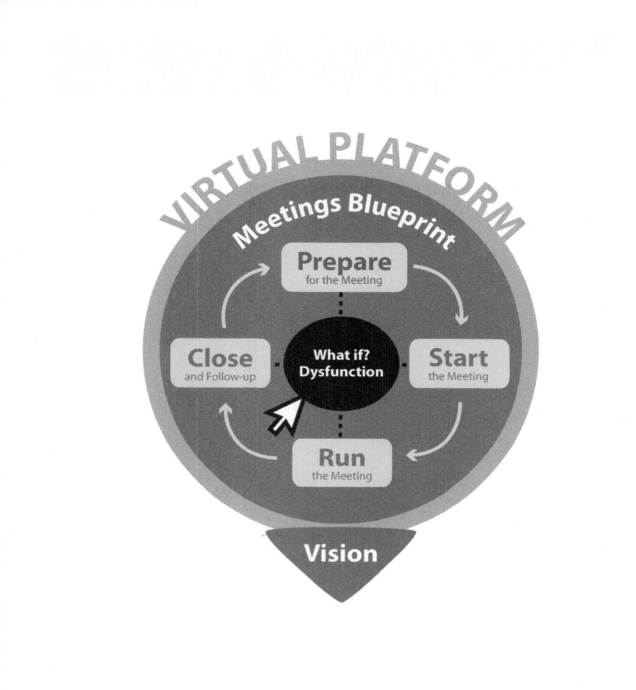

What If There Is Dysfunction? 9

- The Virtual Dilemma
- Conscious Prevention
- Early Detection
- Clean Resolution
- The Angry Exiter
- The Cell Phone Junkie
- The Drop-out
- The Interrupter
- The Late Arriver or Early Leaver
- The Loudmouth
- The Naysayer
- The Process Attacker
- The Storyteller
- The Topic Jumper
- The Verbal Attacker
- The Workaholic
- Group: Low Energy
- Group: Time Pressures
- Back to the Virtual Dilemma
- Summary: The Strategies for Managing Dysfunction

The Virtual Dilemma

It's the second meeting of the performance review task force. As the discussion has progressed to identifying problems with the current performance review process, you've noticed that only a couple of people are contributing. Because participants are not using video for the call you can't see what everyone else is doing. You begin to suspect that some may be multi-tasking or focusing on other work.

You are wondering if you should wait until the next agenda item to address the potential dysfunction or whether you should do something right away. If you do choose to take action, what should you do?

Whether in a virtual meeting or in a face-to-face one, dysfunctional behavior can undermine the meeting's chance of success. We define dysfunctional behavior as follows:

> *Dysfunctional behavior is any activity by a participant that is consciously or unconsciously a substitution for expressing displeasure with the session content or purpose, the facilitation process, or outside factors. Dysfunctional behavior is a symptom, not a root cause.*[13]

There are many different types of dysfunctional behavior that can occur in virtual meetings, ranging from dropping out and not participating to verbally attacking someone and leaving the meeting room in disgust. How do you manage dysfunction in a virtual meeting?

Conscious Prevention

First, we believe that the best dysfunctions are those that don't occur at all. Therefore, we recommend that you preempt dysfunctional behavior before the meeting even begins. During preparation identify participants who might exhibit some form of dysfunctional behavior during the meeting. Specifically, identify the following.

People to Identify in Advance

- People who aren't in favor of holding the meeting
- People who stand to lose something if the meeting is successful
- People who aren't on favorable terms with one another
- People who tend to point out problems rather than solutions

Based on this information, you should take specific action to prevent dysfunction from occurring. The following are four dysfunction prevention strategies that we frequently use.

Dysfunction Prevention Strategies

- **Add ground rules.**
  As indicated in Chapter 4, ground rules provide a vehicle for gaining buy-in to a set of behaviors that will guide how participants interact with one another. As an example, if you learn during preparation that a number of people tend to point out problems rather than solutions, you might add a ground rule: "Make it better." You might describe this by saying, "Let's avoid spending all of our time talking about problems, and focus instead on how to make things better. So if you identify a problem or why something won't work, you have to also come with a solution for how to make it better."

- **Interact with particular people in advance.**
  If there are people who aren't in favor of the meeting or believe they stand to lose something if it is successful, consider having a conversation with them beforehand. During the conversation, you might ask questions such as, "What do you see as the real purpose of the session? What are the problems or issues that will likely surface? How can we ensure that the meeting isn't a waste of time?"

- **Pay close attention to particular reactions.**
  If you are aware that a particular person is not in favor of the meeting or that two people are at odds with each other, you will want to pay close attention to actions and reactions during the virtual meeting. Of course, using a virtual meeting platform that includes video is especially helpful here. For example, if you notice that when a particular person speaks, two people pull back in their seats with expressions of disbelief or disdain, you will want to take action to turn this potentially dysfunctional situation into a functional one. We will cover the best course of action later in this chapter.

- **Use the chat feature to have a private conversation during a break.**
  Breaks are an excellent time to prevent dysfunction by privately discussing issues with people. For example, in the case of the people who pulled back in their seats but did not choose to make a remark, you might engage them separately during the break using the private chat function: "How do you feel the session is going?" or more directly, "I noticed your reaction to Tony's comment. Do you think that what he proposed is a realistic alternative? . . . Your point might be very valid. Would you mind bringing it up to the team so that we will get a number of different views?" The objective, once more, is to encourage functional instead of dysfunctional ways of addressing issues.

Early Detection

Dysfunctional behavior tends to get worse over time if not addressed. What starts out as a mild irritation, if left unaddressed, can lead to passive-aggressive resistance or a direct verbal attack. Why does this occur? One reason is that participants' level of impatience increases with every additional minute that they feel you are wasting their time. Therefore, if you ignore dysfunctional behavior and hope it goes away, you may be setting yourself up for a much larger problem later on.

Accordingly, we recommend that you actively look for these early signs of dysfunction, and should you detect any of them, take action immediately.

Early Signs of Dysfunction

- Participants who are not speaking
- Participants who complain or object publicly to the group
- Participants whose outward expressions seem to indicate that they are not buying in
- Participants whose body language (e.g., folded arms) seems to indicate uneasiness with the session

Warning!

Of course, body language may be difficult to detect even if you are using video during the virtual meeting. In addition, just because people's arms are folded doesn't necessarily mean they are about to become dysfunctional. It could mean the temperature in their room is too cold for them. Over the course of the meeting, however, you will be able to construct an idea of "baseline behaviors" for individuals. You will want to be on the lookout for changes. For example, you will want to notice when, after a comment, someone pulls back from their desk or when people who were smiling and nodding their heads suddenly withdraw.

Clean Resolution

This section focuses on some of the more common dysfunctional behaviors that afflict virtual meetings.[14] How you respond to a dysfunction depends on the dysfunction and other factors, including when it occurs, the number of people affected, and the probable root cause. However, consider the following general formula:

General Formula for Addressing Dysfunction

- Approach the participant privately or generally.

  Either initiate a private chat during a break or address the behaviors generally to the group, being careful not to single out individuals. At times, however, singling someone out during the meeting may be unavoidable.

- Empathize with the symptom.

  Praise an appropriate aspect of their behavior or express concern about their situation.

- Address the root cause.

  Make an effort to get at the real issue by asking a question that will yield a response that confirms the issue.

- Get agreement on the solution.

  Seek agreement on how the situation will be handled going forward. Be sure that the solution addresses the root cause of the dysfunction and not just the symptom.

With each of the common dysfunctions that follow, we have provided a description of the dysfunction, its likely causes, strategies for preventing the dysfunction, what to do "in the moment" when the dysfunction occurs, and what to do "after the moment" to further address the dysfunction. While most are individual dysfunctions, the last two dysfunctions are related to the entire group.

- Angry exiter
- Cell phone junkie
- Dropout
- Interrupter
- Late arriver/early leaver
- Loudmouth
- Naysayer
- Process attacker
- Storyteller
- Topic jumper
- Verbal attacker
- Workaholic
- Group: low energy
- Group: time pressures

Study the various dysfunctions. Understand their common causes, the prevention strategies, and the actions to take in the moment. Advance preparation can help you prevent dysfunction and respond appropriately should the need arise.

The Angry Exiter

Description	The person exits the meeting in apparent disgust.
Common Causes	• The person has an issue unrelated to the meeting that needs immediate attention. • The person does not believe the meeting is worth investing additional time. • The person is dissatisfied with the meeting content or meeting process.
Prevention	• Establish a ground rule: "Everyone speaks about issues in the meeting room; we will discuss the un-discussable."
In the Moment	• "Wow, Bill just exited the meeting. Given what felt like abruptness, I don't think it was because he had to go to the restroom." • "We could try to continue working, but I bet many people are thinking about Bill's departure. So I would like to take a few minutes to get clarity on what just happened. Who can take a shot at explaining what happened and why you think it happened?" • "So we have talked about what happened, and we have a guess as to why it may have happened. Now, I have two other questions. What should we do about Bill? And what needs to happen differently to keep the rest of us from doing what Bill just did?" • By taking a few minutes for debriefing, the group can create a common view of the incident.
After the Moment	• Follow up to ensure that the agreed-upon actions are taken. Consider contacting the person privately yourself.

The Cell Phone Junkie

Description	The person's cell phone constantly rings, or the person is frequently on and off the cell phone.
Common Causes	• The person has a high-priority activity that requires attention during the meeting. • The person is unaware of how phone activity can reduce the effectiveness of the meeting for all participants. • The person sees little value in the meeting and is attempting to make the best of having to be present.
Prevention	• Establish a ground rule: "No phone calls during the meeting."
In the Moment	If a private chat is possible: • "It looks like people don't know you're in an important meeting, so they keep interrupting you. Have you been able to get the problem addressed? Is it okay then to turn the phone off for the rest of the meeting?" If a private conversation is not possible: • "When I heard Tony's phone, it was a reminder to me that we need to keep phones off if we can. I want to check in with the group to make sure this won't be a problem."
After the Moment	• Chat about the issue privately to ensure that no additional problems exist.

The Dropout

Description	The person does not participate in the discussion.
Common Causes	• The person has an introverted communication style and rarely offers comments in a group discussion.
	• The person is typically talkative but is less involved in the discussion because of work pressures or other factors outside of the meeting.
	• The person is dissatisfied with what is being discussed or the way the meeting is being run.
Prevention	• Establish a ground rule: "Everyone speaks."
In the Moment	• "Let's hear from everyone on this next point. With this question, I would like to start with [give the name of a person listed two slots before the dropout] and go down the list. The question is . . ."
	• A round-robin brainstorming activity gets everyone involved. By starting two people before the dropout, you avoid putting the person on the spot and provide the person time to prepare an answer.
After the Moment	• Chat about the issue privately to ensure that no additional problems exist.

The Interrupter

Description	The person interrupts others or finishes their sentences.
Common Causes	• The person agrees with the comment being made, gets excited, and wants to show support. • The person has little patience with the speed at which others speak. • The person feels what he or she has to say is more important or the person disagrees with the comment.
Prevention	• Establish a ground rule: "Have one conversation; respect the speaker."
In the Moment	• "Can you hold that thought for a moment so that the person speaking has the opportunity to finish? It's hard sometimes when you really want to say something, but let's remember our ground rules."
After the Moment	• Chat about the issue privately to ensure that no additional problems exist.

The Late Arriver or Early Leaver

Description	The person habitually arrives late to the meeting or leaves early.
Common Causes	• The person has meetings or other commitments that make it difficult to arrive on time or stay for the entire meeting. • The person does not believe the meeting is worth making full attendance a priority.
Prevention	• Distribute the meeting notice ahead of time. Indicate a gathering time of five to ten minutes before the start time. Indicate that the meeting's purpose and products are important. • Contact the person beforehand to gain commitment to be present for the entire meeting. Get agreement that the meeting should start on time with whoever is present.
In the Moment	• "I want to thank everyone for being here when you could get here and for continuing to do all you can to arrange your schedules so that we can start on time. Our next topic . . ."
After the Moment	• Chat about the issue privately to ensure that no additional problems exist.

The Loudmouth

Description	The person dominates the discussion.
Common Causes	• The person has an extroverted communication style and is not aware that a tendency to frequently speak first can limit the time and opportunity for others to speak. • The person is aware of the tendency and needs help in balancing time spent talking with time spent listening. • The person intentionally wants to dominate in order to limit time spent discussing other views.
Prevention	• Establish a ground rule: "Have one conversation; share the air." • Have a discussion with the person in advance to let the person know that you will be trying to get others to speak. "I appreciate you being willing to speak, especially given that most have been pretty quiet. I need to get other people speaking more so that their views are on the table. So, during this next meeting, there will be times when you might hear me saying, 'Nice point. Let's hear from some others on this.' This way, we'll get everyone's input."
In the Moment	• "Let's hear from everyone on this next point. With this question, I would like to start with [give the name of a person listed after the loudmouth] and go down the list. The question is . . ." • A round-robin brainstorming activity gets everyone involved. By directing the conversation away from the loudmouth, everyone else will be able to provide input first.
After the Moment	• Follow up to ensure that no additional problems exist.

The Naysayer

Description	The person makes audible sighs of displeasure or negative statements such as, "That won't work," without offering solutions.
Common Causes	• The person has a communication style that focuses on identifying problems and risks. • The person opposes the idea suggested and is identifying reasons for the opposition. • The person opposes the idea suggested and is attempting to create stumbling blocks to prevent adoption.
Prevention	• Establish ground rules: "Benefits first (i.e., give the strengths of an idea before identifying problems); take a stand (i.e., rather than describe what won't work, describe what will)."
In the Moment	• Say with optimism, "You may be right. How do we make it better?" • Naysayers often express their views negatively without offering alternatives. Avoid a debate about whether something is wrong by focusing their attention on creating something better.
After the Moment	• Seek to gain agreement to always state benefits before stating problems.

The Process Attacker

Description	The person makes a negative comment about, or requests a change to, the process.
Common Causes	• The person believes the process would be improved by making a change. • The person is uncomfortable with the process or how the meeting leader is handling it. • The person is uncomfortable with the content that is coming out of the process.
Prevention	• During the discussion of ground rules, let the participants know that you will do a process check about halfway through, but if someone has a process recommendation to send a private chat to you to avoid taking up group time.
In the Moment	Actions if a person recommends a process change: • Thank the participant for the suggestion. • Name at least one advantage to the change. • Explain why you believe it may be better to leave things as they are. • Indicate your willingness to following the group's direction. • Ask the group if they agree with the change. (To avoid the perception of bias, do not ask if they agree with leaving things as they are.)
After the Moment	• Following the meeting or during an extended break, have a conversation with the process attacker to ensure there is not an additional problem.

The Storyteller

Description	The person likes to tell long-winded stories.
Common Causes	• The person has an extroverted communication style and is not aware of the tendency to be verbose.
	• The person is aware of the tendency and needs help getting to the point.
	• The person is aware of the tendency and believes each story is worth the group's time and should be completely communicated.
Prevention	• Establish a ground rule: "Share the air."
	• Meet in advance to let the person know that you will have limited discussion time in the meeting.
	"I can see how stories give people a stronger picture of the point you are making. One of the concerns I have is that I've noticed sometimes people drop out when you begin a story. Is there a way that you can make your end point first and then shorten the story so that most will be able to follow? This may also mean that we can get to more things during our meeting. . . . So, during this next meeting, if I perceive that you may be starting a story, you might hear me say, 'Let's give the end point first so that people will be able to follow you better.'"
In the Moment	• "Let's remember the ground rule to give the end point first and keep it brief so that people will be able to follow along better."
After the Moment	• Follow up to ensure that no additional problems exist.

The Topic Jumper

Description	The person frequently takes the group off topic.
Common Causes	• The person has a communication style that frequently shifts to a new topic before the earlier one is complete.
Prevention	• Establish a ground rule: "Have one conversation; one topic at a time."
In the Moment	• "That's an interesting point. If it's okay, can we put that on the issues lists to be discussed later and get back to talking about . . . ?"
After the Moment	• Consider seeking an agreement with the person to use the issues lists when new topics come up.

The Verbal Attacker

Description	The person makes a negative comment about, or directed at, someone.
Common Causes	• Disagreement during the meeting escalates into the verbal attack. • Tensions or issues with a source outside the meeting escalate into a verbal attack during the meeting.
Prevention	• Identify probable issues prior to the meeting. • Establish ground rules: "Discuss the un-discussable; be soft on people but hard on ideas." • Actively keep the conversation focused on seeking solutions rather than assigning blame.
In the Moment	• Interrupt the people if necessary to cut off the debate. Then slow down the discussion and reestablish order. "Let's take a time-out here. We have important issues to discuss, and we have established ground rules to help us do this. One of our ground rules is to be soft on people and hard on ideas. We will unlikely be successful if our focus is on blame. I would like to continue the discussion, if we can, but only if we can do so respectfully and with an understanding of the problems and a focus on developing solutions. Can we do this?"
After the Moment	• Consider taking a break and reconvening the meeting later. • Consider speaking with the parties separately to identify the issues and an appropriate course of action.

The Workaholic

Description	The person does other work during the meeting.
Common Causes	• The person has a high-priority activity that requires attention during the meeting. • The person sees little value in the meeting and is attempting to make the best of having to be present.
Prevention	• Establish a ground rule: "Meeting work only (i.e., during the meeting do work on the meeting only)."
In the Moment	If a private conversation or chat is possible: • "It looks like you have some important work to get done and this meeting has put you in a crunch. We do need your full attention if we can get it. Is this work something you can do later?" If a private conversation is not possible: • "I know we established the ground rule of only doing meeting work while we're here. I want to make sure— does the ground rule still work for everyone?"
After the Moment	• Chat about the issue privately to ensure that no additional problems exist.

Group: Low Energy

Description	Energy in the virtual room is low.
Common Causes	• The group members generally have an introverted communication style and rarely offer comments in a group discussion. • The topic is of low interest to the group, or the speaker or meeting leader is presenting in a low-energy style. • The discussion is occurring during a low-energy period (e.g., right after lunch).
Prevention	• Ensure topics and speakers are appropriate for the audience. • Plan the agenda to use a variety of engagement strategies during low-energy periods.
In the Moment	• During low-energy times, consider using the whip, breakout groups, or round-robins in order to get everyone involved, (e.g., "Let's get everyone's answer to this next question . . .")
After the Moment	• During the evaluation of the meeting, look for other possible reasons for the low energy, such as a lack of interest in the topic.

Group: Time Pressures

Description	You are running out of time.
Common Causes	• The agenda was packed with too many items to cover in the time period. • Too much time during the meeting was spent on items that were of low importance or off-topic.
Prevention	• While reviewing the agenda at the start of the meeting, establish target times for each agenda item. • Put the items that are less critical near the end of the agenda. • Use a timer; alert the group when nearing the scheduled deadline for an item. • Be flexible, allowing additional time when warranted and acceptable to the group, but ending discussions when appropriate.
In the Moment	• "We have hit our time limit with this item. Can we end the discussion here, or do we need additional time? . . . Okay, let's give it an additional five minutes, but let's see if we can wrap it up even sooner." • "It looks like that at the rate we are going, we will not be able to spend the time we need to have a thoughtful discussion on the last agenda item. Does it make sense to move this one to our next meeting, or is there a more appropriate alternative?"
After the Moment	• During the meeting evaluation, look for causes behind the time pressure. Identify ways to tackle more in a single meeting, or to target a more realistic workload within the allotted time.

Back to the Virtual Dilemma

In the virtual dilemma that started the chapter, you suspect that that some of the meeting attendees may be multi-tasking or focusing on other work. The questions we posed were: "Should you wait until the next agenda item to address the potential dysfunction or should you do something right away? If you do choose to take action, what should you do?"

Based on the strategies described in the chapter, you would likely want to address the behavior when it occurs. Assuming that you identified the behavior as dropping out, you would most likely use a round-robin that nudges the dropouts to contribute. Start with a statement such as, "It's important to make sure we have everyone engaged on this." You would then hold a private chat at the break to ensure that there is not an additional problem.

Summary: The Strategies for Managing Dysfunction

In summary, the strategies for managing dysfunction in virtual meetings include the following:

Strategy 51.   Understand the typical dysfunctions that can afflict virtual meetings so that you will be prepared with prevention and response strategies, should the need arise.

Strategy 52.   In general, when responding to dysfunction,

- approach privately or generally,

- empathize with the symptom,

- address the root cause, and

- get agreement on the solution.

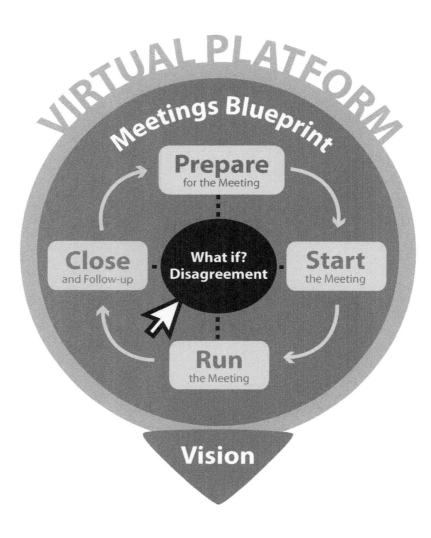

- The Virtual Dilemma
- Defining Agreement
- An Alternative: Five-Finger Consensus
- For Smaller Decisions: Informed Majority
- The Three Reasons People Disagree
- Level 1: Lack of Shared Information
- Level 2: Different Experiences or Values
- Level 3: Outside Factors
- Solving Level 3: Take It to a Higher Source
- Solving Level 1: Delineation
- Solving Level 2: Strengths, Weaknesses, Merging
- Back to the Virtual Dilemma
- Summary: The Strategies for Gaining Agreement

The Virtual Dilemma

Imagine this: The third virtual meeting on improving the performance review process has been going great. The participants are all engaged and the group is making significant progress. But suddenly, with little warning, a major disagreement erupts. One faction believes it is important to slow down and investigate how other organizations are doing performance reviews. Others don't want any delay that could prevent a new process from being in place for the upcoming performance review cycle. Voices get louder, people stop listening, and you sense that the majority of the group may be checking out. You know you have to take control and help the group move to agreement. What do you do?

What process do you use to get the group to consensus?

This chapter will equip you with an understanding of the three reasons people disagree and five techniques for getting to yes when disagreements occur. Let's start by defining agreement.

Defining Agreement

When is a decision a decision? When do you know you have adequate agreement and can move on? You should decide, or have the group decide, the method for decision making. What follows are several alternative methods for decision making:

Leader decides	The group will discuss the strengths and weaknesses of various alternatives, and the leader will make the final decision.
Leader holds veto rights	The group will come to a decision based on one of the methods that follow, but the leader reserves the right to overrule.
Majority rules	The decision is determined by a majority vote. Majority decision making can be quick; however, it can also lead to less-than-optimal solutions and less-than-effective implementation because of limited discussion time and inadequate buy-in.
Super-majority	The group debates until a large majority of the participants agrees with one alternative. The supermajority is often 60 percent, 67 percent, or 75 percent. However, supermajority can also lead to limited discussion and less buy-in.
Full consensus	Consensus encourages discussion until solutions are acceptable to everyone. While consensus increases buy-in, it can also result in watered-down solutions in order to gain full agreement. Additionally, full consensus can take considerably more time.

An Alternative: Five-Finger Consensus

As an alternative to the five decision-making methods above, we have found five-finger consensus to be far more helpful to groups. Here is how five-finger consensus works:

Steps in Five-Finger Consensus

- **Once an idea is proposed, the meeting leader guides the discussion until the group appears ready to check for agreement.** The meeting leader then explains that during the round-robin that follows, each person should give a number from one to five indicating the level of support for the recommendation as shown in Figure 10.1.

Figure 10.1: Five-Finger Consensus

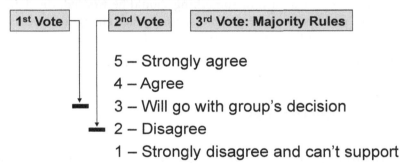

Five-Finger Consensus

- **In the first vote, if everyone indicates five, four, or three, consensus has been reached, and you can move on.** Those who give a five or a four are in full support and those who give a three have indicated they are willing to support the group's decision. If there are any ones or twos, however, those who indicate such should be given the opportunity to explain their rating and recommend alternatives. The champion of the original idea then has the option to make changes or leave the option as it is, and explains his or her decision to the rest of the group. If a change is made to the original idea, then the meeting leader takes the group through a new first vote. If no change is made, however, then the meeting leader takes the second vote.

- **In the second vote, if everyone indicates five, four, three, or two, the decision is made**, and you move ahead. Those who give a two are expressing disagreement with the idea, but also that they won't block the rest of the group from adopting it. If there are any ones, however, those who indicate such are given an additional opportunity to explain their rating and make recommendations to alter the idea. Once more, the idea's champion has the option to make changes or leave the option as it is, and should explain his or her decision to the group. If a change is made, it is new first vote. If no change is made, then the meeting leader takes the third vote.

- **With the third vote, majority rules**. The decision is made based on a majority of the participants.

Five-finger consensus encourages the group to listen carefully when there is disagreement, and it encourages listening carefully twice, if necessary, so that those in disagreement have at least two opportunities to express their concerns. In the end, however, the will of the group is allowed to prevail. Perhaps as important, five-finger consensus also avoids the tendency to water down ideas that have the support of most of the group, in the name of reaching full consensus.

For Smaller Decisions: Informed Majority

For significant group decisions, such as determining key priorities, changing the direction of a project, or adopting a mission statement, we recommend five-finger consensus. For smaller decisions, such as three options for how something should be worded, the date to set for a specific milestone, the number to set for a target, or a suggested change to a recommendation, we have coined the phrase "informed majority" to describe the process we recommend.

Let's use the instance of three suggestions for how something should be worded. Informed majority works as follows.

The Informed Majority Process

Gather all alternatives.	"We have at this point three alternatives for how to word this recommendation. Are there any other alternatives?"
Ask someone to speak for each alternative.	"Okay, let's go back now and have someone speak for each alternative. If no one speaks for the alternative, it will go away as an option. So the first alternative is . . . Would someone speak for it? If not it goes away as an option . . . The second alternative is . . ."
Ask for additional comments.	"Now that we have had one person speak for each alternative, are there any other comments anyone would like to make?"
Call for the vote.	"Now that we are informed, it's time to vote. All those in favor of the first alternative . . ."

Hold a runoff, if needed.	If there are multiple alternatives and no alternative receives a majority of votes, then all but the top two alternatives are dropped and a re-vote is taken.

In cases where there is a recommendation to make a change and the only other alternative is to not make the change, you can make a small adjustment to the process. In Step 2 say, "Would someone speak for making the change? Now would someone speak against making the change? If no one speaks against it, then there is no need to vote and the change will be made by default."

The goal of informed majority is to make minor decisions in an efficient and effective manner, while ensuring that all voices are heard and time is given to create and discuss alternatives.

The Three Reasons People Disagree

Disagreements generally occur for one of three reasons:[15]

- Level 1: There is a lack of shared information.
- Level 2: People have different values or experiences.
- Level 3: Outside factors are affecting the disagreement.

Let's look first at each of the three levels of disagreement and then at methods for resolving each one.

Level 1: Lack of Shared Information

In a Level 1 disagreement, the dissenters have not clearly heard or understood each other's alternatives and the reasons for supporting them. Level 1 disagreements are often a result of an assumed understanding of what the other person is saying or meaning. Take a look at the sample below.

Sample Dialogue: Level 1 Disagreement

Pepper: I've been thinking about the problems we have been having with our performance review process, and I think I've come up with a solution: We should have our employees write their own reviews.

Michelle: Are you out of your mind? That can't work.

Pepper: Sure it can. You said yourself that most supervisors can't remember all the things their employees did in the prior year, and you said that last time, most of the reviews were superficial and based mostly on favoritism or on the last project people did. If employees write their own performance reviews, the focus will be on how people actually performed the entire year.

Michelle: No, I don't think so. Pepper, we have been partners for some time. But this has to be the craziest idea you have come up with in a while.

Pepper: I don't understand why you don't like it.

Michelle: Well, can you say, "Fox guarding the hen house"? If we let people write their own performance reviews, every review will be rated "far exceeds expectations." People won't admit their failures. Plus, this approach completely disempowers the managers. The performance review is an opportunity for managers to influence the performance of their people. Letting employees rate themselves eliminates this. And what about—

Pepper: Hold on a second. I'm not sure you are hearing me. I said have the employees write their performance reviews, not determine their ratings. That's their manager's job. But if we have the employees write about their own accomplishments, strengths, and—

Michelle: And their areas for improvement. I get it. Then you have the manager review what the employee wrote and make additions and changes as needed with the employee in the room. Then the manager sets the rating. That makes sense. But why didn't you say that in the first place?

Pepper: I did say it. You just weren't listening. I said I wanted employees to write their performance reviews. What did you think I meant?

It's fairly evident what Michelle thought Pepper meant. When Pepper said, "We should have our employees write their own reviews," Michelle thought Pepper wanted to have employees set their own ratings. Once Michelle understood what Pepper meant, they quickly realized they were in agreement.

Unfortunately, many Level 1 disagreements are not resolved as quickly. People often argue without realizing that they actually agree. This condition occurs so frequently that there is a name for it: **violent agreement**. When a Level 1 disagreement is resolved, you will often hear, "Oh, is that what you meant? Why didn't you say that?"

Level 2: Different Experiences or Values

In a Level 2 disagreement, the parties have fully heard and understood one another's alternatives. However, they have had different experiences or hold different values that result in affinity for one idea over another. The sample that follows describes what appears to be a Level 2 disagreement, at least on the surface.

Sample Dialogue: Level 2 Disagreement

Terry: If we are going to have any chance of transforming the meetings around here, we need to get everyone trained on what a great virtual meeting is and how to create it. I understand there is a company that has courses on Facilitating Virtual Meetings and I think we need to get everyone in training as soon as possible.

Jordan: Everyone in training? Surely you're kidding. We can't train everyone in our organization. Maybe just the executives and managers. They are the ones who actually lead meetings.

Terry: No, we can't limit this. It's not just the executives and managers who lead meetings. And just about everyone participates in one or more meetings every week. Everyone needs these skills. Everyone should take the course.

Jordan: When we do training, it has to be focused on the people who will get the most out of it. It never ceases to amaze me how you folks in HR want to get everybody involved in everything. You all need to keep in mind that this is a business. Training is an expense, not revenue, and it hurts revenue when you take people away from their real jobs.

Terry: Don't lecture me. I know about finances. The problem is that you guys in the field don't have a clue about what it means to empower people. If you took the time to make people feel like a part of the organization, you might be able to keep them for more than eighteen months.

This disagreement is going downhill fast. On the surface, it looks like a classic clash of perspectives, with the person in the field valuing operations and the human resources representative valuing people. We will come back to this disagreement later in the chapter.

Level 3: Outside Factors

A Level 3 disagreement is based on personality, past history, or other outside factors that have nothing to do with the alternatives.

Sample Dialogue: Level 3 Disagreement

Sean: If our team is going to be successful in making major improvements to our performance review process, we should look at three to seven organizations known to do it well and identify their best practices.

Chris: That's a stupid idea. There is no way that will work.

Sean: Sure it will. We did something similar where I last worked. We just need to make sure we identify the right organizations.

Chris: No, it won't work.

Sean: I don't understand why you are being so difficult.

Chris: Because it won't work.

Leader: You may be right, Chris. It might not work. So what do we have to do to make it work?

Chris: There's nothing we can do. It just won't work.

Leader: Okay. . . . Well, how about explaining what's wrong with it?

Chris: Everything is wrong with it. It just won't work.

Leader: Help us understand, Chris. Why are you so convinced it won't work?

Chris: It just won't work. He thought of it. It won't work!

As you can detect from this example, the problem Chris has with the best practices idea doesn't seem to have much to do with the idea at all. Chris appears to believe that the problem is Sean, the person offering the idea. As it turns out, Chris learned some time ago that when he was interviewing to join the organization, Sean was one of the few people not in favor of hiring him. Since then, Chris has disagreed with Sean's judgment in almost everything.

Solving Level 3: Take It to a Higher Source

Level 3 disagreements are based on outside factors. Therefore, you can waste considerable time if you try to solve the disagreement by analyzing the issue or identifying alternatives, because the disagreement does not concern either.

To avoid wasting time on Level 3 issues, recognize the two signs that tend to indicate that a disagreement is Level 3.

Signs of a Level 3 Disagreement	• Irrational arguments • No interest in considering or discussing alternatives

How do you resolve a Level 3 disagreement? Take it to a higher source. The following example uses the scenario from the earlier section featuring Chris and Sean.

Sample Dialogue: Resolving a Level 3 Disagreement

Agree to disagree.	"Chris and Sean, can we agree that we are not going to agree on this point?"
Gain agreement to take it to a higher source.	"I would like to suggest the following: Let's the three of us hold a virtual meeting with the vice president of human resources. Sean, explain what you want to do. Chris, you will have the opportunity to explain your concerns. And we'll let the VP decide what happens next."
Consider having a private conversation with the dissenter to identify the core issue. Use the dysfunction resolution approach from the previous chapter.	"I appreciate all the skills you bring to the team, especially when you are giving recommendations on how to fix things. I've noticed on a few occasions that you have disagreed strongly with suggestions from Sean. Tell me more about this. . . . Is there something I should do differently as the meeting leader? . . . Is there something up with you and Sean that may be getting in the way?"

Solving Level 1: Delineation

If the disagreement does not demonstrate Level 3 signs (i.e., irrationality or no commitment to finding a solution), it is typically best to begin addressing the disagreement as if it were Level 1: assume that all the key information is not necessarily known by all parties. Use techniques that slow down the conversation in order to encourage careful listening and comprehension. Consider the following steps.

The Delineation Steps

1.	Start with agreement.	"We seem to all agree that . . ."
2.	Confirm the source of the disagreement.	"Where we seem to disagree is . . . Is that right?"
3.	Identify the alternatives.	"So, Terry, you are saying . . . And, Sean, you are saying . . ."
4.	Ask each party specific questions to delineate the alternative.	"How would this work? How much? How long? Who is involved in . . . ? What is involved in . . . ?"
5.	Summarize the information.	"Based on what Terry has said, this alternative will cost . . . And it will take . . . And, as a result, we will have . . . Based on what Sean has said . . ."
6.	Take a consensus check.	"Based on what we have discussed so far, how many would be in favor of . . . and how many in favor of . . ."

Through delineation you encourage each party to listen carefully to one another. When the disagreement stems only from a lack of shared information, the parties quickly learn that they did not disagree at all. Either they did not hear each other, heard but did not understand each other, or did not share relevant information.

As the meeting leader, you get them to hear one another by taking them through the delineation steps. As a result of delineation, everyone in the meeting should know the answers for each alternative to the following delineation questions.

The Delineation Questions	• How much . . . ?
	• How long . . . ?
	• Who is involved in . . . ?
	• What is involved in . . . ?

During the delineation, we recommend gathering the new information on a whiteboard or in an application through desktop sharing to allow all meeting participants to see it. Recording the information helps improve the group's understanding and increases engagement.

The sample dialogue that follows continues the disagreement between Terry and Jordan concerning who should take the meetings training. The dialogue picks up with Terry's last comment.

Sample Dialogue: Level 1 Disagreement Resolved

Terry: Don't lecture me. I know about finances. The problem is that you guys in the field don't have a clue what it means to empower people. If you took the time to make people feel like a part of the organization, you might be able to keep them for more than eighteen months.

Leader: Let's slow down for a minute. It seems like you both agree that meeting training could help us, is that right?

Terry: Definitely.

Leader: Where you seem to disagree is on who should take the course?

Jordan: That's right.

Leader: So, Terry, you are saying that everyone should take the course.

Terry: That's right. (Leader labels the first column "Everyone.")

Leader: And, Jordan, you are saying something different?

Jordan: Yes, I think only key managers should take the class. (Leader labels the second column "Key Managers.")

Leader: Terry, you said everyone would take the meetings course. How would it work? How many people is that?

Terry: All six hundred of our employees.

Leader: Would each one take the full three-day course?

Terry: No. I would want the vendor to create a special half-day class for our people so that they wouldn't have to spend so much time away from work.

Jordan: A half-day course? Why didn't you say that? I have no problem with that. We can make that work.

In this case, Terry and Jordan were in "violent agreement." They were arguing because they had made assumptions about what the other had meant. Delineation solves this.

But what if Terry really meant a three-day course? Figure 10.2 provides a sample of what a meeting leader might record during the virtual meeting as a result of the delineation steps.

Figure 10.2: Results from Delineation

Results from Delineation	
Everyone	**Key Managers Only**
600 people	100 people
Sign up by team	Execs select managers
3-day class	3-day class
20 people/class	20 people/class
32 classes	6 classes (one makeup)
4 classes/month	2 classes/month
$18,000/class	$18,000/class
600 people	100 people
8 months	3 months
$576,000	$108,000

At this point, Sean and Terry understand one another's ideas but are still in disagreement. In this case, you would conclude that this is not a Level 1 disagreement and would begin using Level 2 resolution strategies, which follow.

Solving Level 2: Strengths, Weaknesses, Merging

If consensus has not been reached through delineation, the disagreement may be a Level 2 conflict based on different values or experiences. You solve a Level 2 disagreement by identifying the strengths and weaknesses of each idea and checking for consensus. If agreement is not reached, you then have the group identify the key strengths of each idea and then create an alternative that combines the key strengths. The steps follow.

The Steps for Solving a Level 2 Disagreement

1. Identify the strengths.	"Let's take a look at each idea starting with the first one. What are the strengths of this idea?"
2. Identify the weaknesses.	"Now that we have identified the strengths of each idea, let's look at the weaknesses. What are the weaknesses of this first idea?"
3. Take a consensus check.	"Based on these strengths and weaknesses, how many now would be in favor of . . . And how many in favor of . . ."
4. Identify key strengths.	"Let's look at each idea again and identify their one or two most important strengths."
5. Create one or more new alternatives.	"Is there an alternative that might combine these key strengths?"
6. Delineate the top alternative.	"Let's delineate this new alternative to ensure that we all understand. How much . . ."
7. Take a consensus check.	"Based on what we have discussed thus far, how many would be in favor of . . . ?"

When you ask people the strengths of an idea, their responses typically represent the values they hold that result in them preferring their idea over the other. In our example, those who prefer the "train everyone" idea place greater value on common language and universal benefit. Those who prefer the "key managers only" idea place greater value on saving money and limiting time away from work.

The merging process encourages the group to create an alternative that combines the key values of all the participants. Figure 10.3 provides a sample of what a meeting leader might record during a virtual meeting using the merge process with the training course disagreement between Sean and Terry (described earlier).

Figure 10.3: Results from Merge

Results from Merge	
Everyone	**Key Managers**
<u>Strengths</u>	<u>Strengths</u>
Common language*	Less expensive*
Everyone benefits	Completed more quickly
Skills throughout the organization*	Less time away from work*
	Training focused on those who need it

* Key strengths

<u>New Alternative</u>
Provide a three-day course for key managers and a half-day overview for all employees.

Back to the Virtual Dilemma

So, what do you do when disagreement breaks out? Recall that the disagreement occurred because some believe it is important to slow down and investigate how other organizations are doing performance reviews. Others don't want any delay that could prevent a new process from being in place for the upcoming performance review cycle.

Resolution Approach

1.	First, rule out Level 3.	Recall that the telltale signs of a Level 3 are that the arguments are irrational and there is no interest in discussing alternatives. In this particular case, it appears that the two alternatives are quite rational.
2.	Then start with agreement.	"We seem to all agree that we want to improve our current performance review process."

3.	Confirm the source of the disagreement.	"Where we seem to disagree is whether we should take the time to get input from other organizations, is that right?"
4.	Identify the ideas.	"So, Sharon, you are saying we should seek input from other organizations before moving forward. And, Marsha, you are saying it is important to have the new system in place before the next performance review cycle and taking the time to seek input from other organizations could jeopardize the timing. Again, do I have that right?"
5.	Delineate the ideas by asking each party specific questions related to how much, how long, who is involved, and what is involved.	"Okay, so Sharon, if we were to seek input from other organizations, how would that work? How would we go about getting the input? From how many organizations would we seek input? How long do you think it would take? Who would have to be involved in making it happen?" "Now, Marsha, if we didn't seek input, what would we do instead? How would that work? How long do you think it would take? Who would have to be involved in making it happen?"
6.	Summarize the information.	"Based on what Sharon has said, this idea will cost . . . And the amount of time it will take is . . . And, as a result, we will have . . . Based on what Marsha has said . . ."
7.	Take a consensus check.	"Based on what we have discussed thus far, how many would be in favor of . . . and how many in favor of . . . ?"

Note that at this point, this disagreement might be resolved. For example, if through delineation, Sharon explained that she envisions a brief, two-week process for seeking information from other organizations and that even with the delay we would still meet the deadline for incorporating into the next performance cycle by thirty days, the disagreement would most likely be resolved—so, Level 1.

Alternatively, if through delineation Marsha explained that we had no room for delay if the team wanted to meet this year's performance review cycle and that instead we could use a best practices study of performance reviews done last year by an international human resource management association, once more, the disagreement would most likely be resolved—so, also Level 1.

If, however, delineation did not solve the disagreement, the leader would conclude that this was a Level 2 disagreement and then use strengths, weaknesses, and merge process as described earlier in this chapter.

Summary: The Strategies for Gaining Agreement

In summary, the strategies for gaining agreement in virtual meetings include the following:

Strategy 53.   Early on, decide how decisions will be made.

Strategy 54.   Use five-finger consensus as a decision-making vehicle to gain a broad base of agreement without jeopardizing the quality of a solution, as often happens when unanimous support is sought.

Strategy 55.   Use informed majority for less significant decisions to help ensure relevant information is discussed.

Strategy 56.   When faced with a disagreement, determine whether the disagreement is Level 1 (information), 2 (values or experience), or 3 (personality, past history, or other outside factors).

Strategy 57.   Apply the appropriate consensus building strategy—delineation, strengths-weaknesses-merging, or higher source—depending on the level of the disagreement.

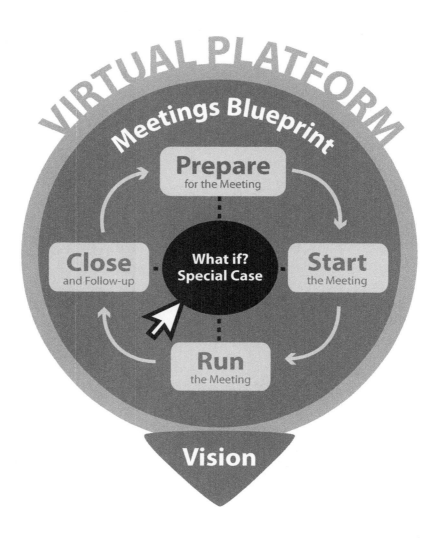

What If the Meeting Is a
Special Virtual Case?

11

- The Virtual Dilemma

- What If Only a Few People Are Remote?

- What If a Large Number of People Are Remote?

- What If You Are the Only Person Not in the Room?

- Summary: The Strategies for Special Virtual Cases

The Virtual Dilemma

In the final meeting of the performance review task force, the team decides to come together for a face-to-face, half-day session to wrap up the project. Unfortunately, of the seven members, one can't make it and will have to connect virtually while all the other team members will be together in the same room.

While you have become quite adept at running virtual meetings where nearly all of the participants are remote, what do you do now when only one is? What changes do you make? What do you have to do differently?

How do you run a virtual meeting when most of the participants are in the same room and only a few are remote?

As indicated in the first chapter, this book fully describes strategies for virtual meetings from the perspective of the extreme case in which you and most of the participants are in different locations. There are, however, virtual meetings in which this is not the case. This chapter, adapted from *The Secrets of Facilitation*,[16] focuses on three special virtual cases, as follows.

- What if only a few people are remote?
- What if a large number of people are remote?
- What if you are the only person not in the room?

What If Only a Few People Are Remote?

Frequently in virtual meetings there are only one or two people remote and the rest of the participants are together in the same room with you. Unfortunately, when this is the case, the meeting leader can easily forget about the remote participants. In addition, because there are only a few of them, remote participants can easily feel isolated and uninvolved.

We recommend using the following strategies to increase engagement and involvement when there are only a few people remote.

Recommended Strategies

- Since there will be only a few remote participants, it is easy to forget that these people will not be in the room to receive handouts. Make it a point to send the agenda and all handouts to remote participants before the meeting.

- If possible, choose a virtual meeting platform that allows for video. Have a webcam of the meeting room and project the video of the remote participants on a screen in the main room.

- When information would normally be recorded on flip charts, consider recording the information using the virtual meeting platform; for example, via desktop sharing or whiteboarding, so the remote participants can see the information.

- Add a ground rule, "Don't lose the remote." We explain the ground rule in the following way:

  "We have a few people who are remote and not in the room with us. It is important that we treat them as if they are in the room. We don't want to lose the remote. So we want to consistently request their input. We want to consistently keep them engaged. In the same way, remote participants, we want to give you the option to chime in at any time to get my attention as the meeting leader. And so whatever we do, we don't want to lose the remote."

- Consider always starting first with the remote participants when asking a question. By starting with them first every time, it is less likely that they will be overlooked.

- Should you not want to start each time with the remote participants, a different strategy is to have a name card and chair at the table for each of the remote participants. When round-robins are used, the name card will prompt you to ask for comments from the remote participants.

- When using breakout groups be sure to have a way to assign a breakout group to the few who are remote. If you have an adequate number of remote participants (at least two, but no more than eight), you might consider assigning all remote members to a separate team and have someone in the room serve as that team's recorder.

What If a Large Number of People Are Remote?

As indicated in Chapter 4, we recommend that you plan to have a significant interactive activity at least once every ten to twenty minutes in a virtual meeting. This frequency of interaction is necessary to maintain high engagement during virtual meetings, since the temptation to check out might be great.

Three of the most common engagement activities include the following:

- Round-robins in which the meeting leader calls the participants by name to have them respond in turn to a question

- Whiteboarding in which all members of the team simultaneously type responses

- The whip, which, similar to round-robins, has everyone respond to a question. The whip is intended to be a very quick temperature check, though, so participants are typically restricted to a one- to three-word response.

If there are more than sixteen or so people who are remote, the whip can become tedious going through all the names, round-robins can take far too long, and a whiteboard can become congested and completely cluttered with responses. When you have a large number of remote participants, we recommend the following strategies.

Recommended Strategies

- Divide the group into teams, with as many teams as needed to limit the size of each team to four or five people. Consider creating a single slide with the names of the people on each team, which you can pull up from time to time as a visual reminder.

- When you would normally do a round-robin by person, do a round-robin by team, allowing anyone from the team to respond.

- When you do whiteboarding, consider having half or fewer of the teams type information on the whiteboard in response to a question. Once all information is typed, do a round-robin with the teams that did not participate and ask for any additions.

- Make much greater use of polls, which typically engage everyone.

What If You Are the Only Person Not in the Room?

As with the case study that ended the first chapter, there may be times when all the attendees are present in a single room, but the meeting leader is in a different location. This happens frequently to us as professional facilitators when we are guiding a client's remote team. Internal and external consultants, team coaches, project managers, business analysts, architects, and others in the professional services arenas may more and more find themselves in this position as virtual meetings become even more pervasive.

Being the meeting leader and the only one remote is especially difficult because, along with all the other typical challenges with virtual meetings, you usually can't see the group dynamics that everyone else can! For example, you can't see the body language that says the group is getting frustrated with a topic, but everyone else can. You can't see that people are confused with the directions you are giving, but everyone else can. You can't see when the group has lost interest in your long monologue, but everyone else can.

To help minimize the impact of your not being in the room, we recommend the following.

Recommended Strategies

- If possible, choose a virtual meeting platform that allows for video. Have a webcam centered on the meeting room, and have a screen at the front of the room onto which you're projected.

- If people will be working around tables in separate teams, consider having a webcam and audio for each table that shows the people at that table, which allows you to observe, and comment if necessary, on the interaction. The audio may allow you to turn on or mute individual tables. This will likely require some testing to reduce annoying feedback echoes and screeches.

- Ask someone to serve as your eyes in the room. Ask this person to point out those things that you can't see. Let the person know that you are looking to him or her to point out what the group may be feeling, when the group appears to be in agreement, or when there is a need to speed up or slow down.

- If the group has more than four or five tables, one person serving as your eyes may not be enough. Consider asking a person at each table to play this role.

- Use the virtual meeting platform as your primary tool for documenting all pertinent information during the session so that everyone can see the information.

- If breakout groups will be using flip charts, consider assigning a separate recorder to each breakout group who records the information electronically into a pre-formatted template. When it is time for the teams to report back, you can project the recorded information onto the main screen through the virtual meeting platform so everyone, and you, can see it.

Summary: The Strategies for Special Virtual Cases

In summary, the strategies for addressing virtual meetings that present special issues include the following.

Strategy 58. If only a few people are remote, use the ground rule, "Don't lose the remote," and be sure to include remote participants throughout the meeting by starting with them first.

Strategy 59. If a large number of people are remote, divide the group into teams; use round-robins by team; ask every member of half or fewer of the teams to specifically respond in each activity.

Strategy 60. If you are the only person not in the room, choose a virtual meeting platform that allows for video, assign someone to serve as your eyes in the room, and consider webcams at every table so you can observe the interaction.

- Chapter 12. Pulling It All Together

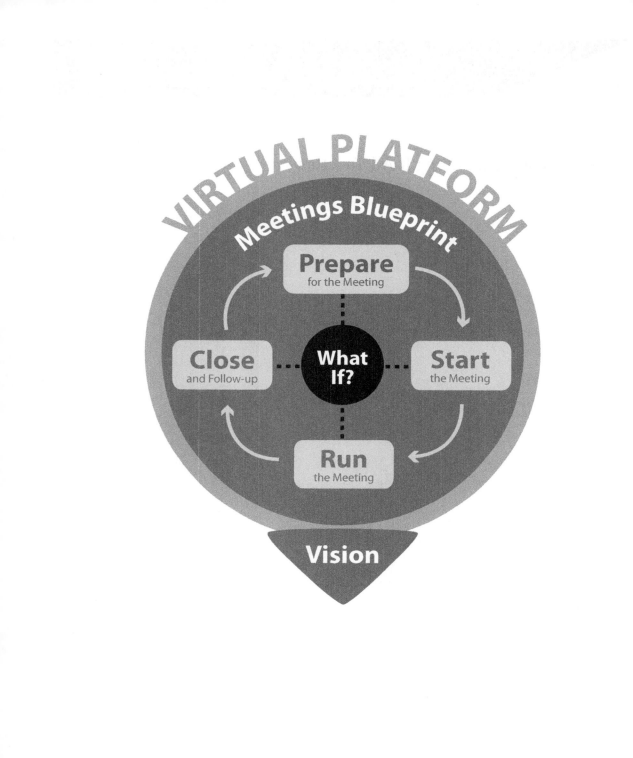

12 Pulling It All Together

- Preparing
- Starting the Meeting
- Running the Meeting
- Closing the Meeting
- A Final Word

This book contains sixty strategies for running highly engaging and highly interactive virtual meetings. In this chapter we demonstrate how to put the tools and techniques together in the preparation, start, execution, and close of a two-hour virtual meeting. For our meeting, let's use the example that has been described periodically throughout the book, the first meeting of the virtual team on improving the performance review process.

Preparing

As you recall from Chapter 4, planning and preparing for a highly interactive and engaging virtual meeting typically requires more time than planning for a face-to-face meeting. To prepare for this meeting, let's use the Checklist for Preparing that appears at the beginning of Chapter 4.

Figure 12.1: Checklist for Preparing

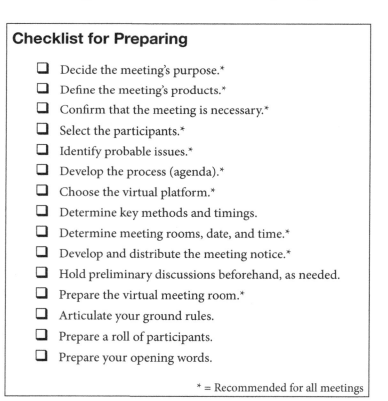

Checklist for Preparing

❑ Decide the meeting's purpose.*
❑ Define the meeting's products.*
❑ Confirm that the meeting is necessary.*
❑ Select the participants.*
❑ Identify probable issues.*
❑ Develop the process (agenda).*
❑ Choose the virtual platform.*
❑ Determine key methods and timings.
❑ Determine meeting rooms, date, and time.*
❑ Develop and distribute the meeting notice.*
❑ Hold preliminary discussions beforehand, as needed.
❑ Prepare the virtual meeting room.*
❑ Articulate your ground rules.
❑ Prepare a roll of participants.
❑ Prepare your opening words.

* = Recommended for all meetings

Please Note

In the pages that follow, we take you through a very thorough preparation process. In the case of the performance review improvement meeting, we want the session to be a knock-your-socks-off virtual meeting and therefore we carefully cover *every item* in the preparation checklist. As you can see, the checklist includes some items that are asterisked, indicating they should be done for every virtual meeting, and some items that are not. You may find that the level of thorough planning demonstrated in this section is not required for all or even most of your meetings. Our goal is to provide you with a solid example of thorough planning and preparation, which you can choose how to best use.

Decide the meeting's purpose	The purpose of this first meeting of the performance review task force is to kick off the virtual team you will be leading. You want to ensure that every member is clear on what is to be achieved, how the team is going to achieve it, and the individual roles in making it happen.
Define the meeting's products	<ul><li>The team's definition of success</li><li>Group norms</li><li>Work process</li><li>Meetings and logistics plan</li><li>Communications plan</li></ul>
Confirm the meeting is necessary	<ul><li>Is it possible to achieve the purpose and products without a meeting? (No)</li><li>Are the purpose and products worth the time and resources that the meeting will consume? (Yes)</li></ul>
Select the participants	You have six additional team members, one from each region selected by the regional vice president. While you and one other are based in the Atlanta headquarters, the other five team members are based in Boston, Chicago, Dallas, Denver, and San Diego. In addition, your team members include two individual contributors, two supervisors, two mid-level managers, and a senior manager. The team also cuts across the departments and major business functions. Because they each have other duties, team members have agreed to give up to 10 percent of their time a week (four hours) to the task force.
Identify probable issues	<ul><li>There is likely to be some skepticism concerning whether management will be willing to change.</li><li>There will be pressure to ensure the team finishes within sixty days so as to influence the upcoming performance review cycle.</li><li>The team covers four time zones; therefore, we should pay close attention to scheduling and communicating meeting times.</li></ul>

Develop the process (agenda)	• You decide to use a modified version of the agenda for "The First Meeting of a Task Force" described in *The Secrets of Facilitation*.[17] A. Welcome, charge, deliverables, meeting's purpose B. Key topics and questions C. Agenda D. Meeting ground rules and parking boards E. Gifts and hooks F. Our definition of success G. Proposed work process H. Team norms I. Operating logistics J. Review and next steps K. Evaluation and close
Choose the virtual platform	While you are more familiar with the GoToMeeting system, you choose to use the WebEx platform for the team, primarily due to its benefit of simultaneous typing provided through the whiteboard feature.
Determine key methods and timings	Deciding what methods to use is a critical step in planning an engaging meeting. The information that follows describes a helpful thought process. A time estimate for each agenda item appears in the left column. As indicated in Chapter 5, you should **prepare a starting question in advance** for each agenda item that requests numerous responses from the participants.
2 min.	A. Welcome, charge, deliverables, meeting's purpose • Present information about what we have been asked to do, our overall deliverables, and the specific purpose for this meeting (PowerPoint).

8 min.	B. Key topics and questions

- Do a round-robin (starting with the first name in the roll call list) to collect issues.

- **Starting question**: "Think about our charge and deliverables, and imagine the steps we might take in getting it done. Think about the questions you have about what we are being asked to do or how we are going to go about doing it. Think about the ideas you have or the topics you know we need to discuss. Let's build a list. As we start this project, what are the questions or key topics you would like to see discussed?"

- Record in the meeting notes document (Word).

10 min.	C. Agenda

- Have a preloaded poll to accept the agenda.

- Review the agenda (PowerPoint).

- Split the screen to show both the agenda and issues.

- Pair into three subgroups.

- Alternately ask subgroups to identify where each topic and question will be discussed.

- Record the agenda letter at the front of each topic so you can sort by agenda letter.

- Use the preloaded poll to ask the group to accept the agenda.

5 min.

D. Meeting ground rules and parking boards

- Have a preloaded poll to accept the ground rules.

- Review your prepared ground rules (PowerPoint).

- Explain that you will be leading the meeting and giving your comments as well.

- Use a round-robin (starting with the second person in the list) and ask for additions or changes.

- **Starting question**: "Think about meetings you have been in before, either in our organization or others. Think about the kinds of behaviors you've seen people do that you think are unproductive or unacceptable; behaviors you want to make sure don't happen within this team. What are additional ground rules you might want to add?"

- Record in the meeting notes document (Word).

- Use the preloaded poll to formally ask the team to adopt the meeting ground rules.

- Review the parking boards (PowerPoint).

10 min. | E. Gifts and hooks

- Show the definition of gifts (things the team member brings that can help the team achieve its objectives) and hooks (what has to happen to keep the team member engaged and coming back) (Whiteboard).

- Give team members two minutes to record three gifts and one hook on the formatted whiteboard.

- **Starting question**: "Given our charge and deliverables, each of us brings certain gifts to this work, certain skills, experiences, attributes, or resources that will help the team be successful. Think about your gifts. Think about the things that you have that will help the team achieve its goals. In addition, you know what needs to happen to keep you engaged. You know what needs to be going on that will make you excited about continuing to be a part of the team. What is the most important thing that needs to be going on to keep you hooked? Please record on the whiteboard three gifts you bring and one hook."

- Have team members explain their three gifts and one hook, starting with the first name in the roll call list.

- Copy the gifts and hooks in the meeting notes document following the meeting (Word).

10 min.

F. Our definition of success

- Present the three standard measures of success (project targets, business result targets, satisfaction targets) with samples. Also explain the difference between yardsticks and targets (PowerPoint).

- Use round-robin brainstorming (starting with the third person in the list) to have the team brainstorm the yardsticks—first at the end of the project, and then one year later.

- Record everything in the meeting notes document (Word). Use a split screen to show samples while recording.

- **Starting question**: "Let's imagine that we are at the end of the project and it has been a resounding success. How would we know? Think about the things that would tell us we were successful as we are ending the project, things that show we did a great job. Consider the three categories on the screen. What would tell us we have been successful?"

- **Starting question**: "Now let's imagine that the project is done and we have just completed a full year with the new performance review process. And once more, it's been an amazing success. For this first measure, think about the target that would indicate that we have been successful. What is that target?"

- Use informed majority to decide which of the yardsticks to use.

- After the yardsticks are decided, have the team determine the specific target for each yardstick by using subgroups (Word).

20 min.	G. Proposed work process

- Show the standard process improvement work process (Word).

- Use a split screen between the standard process improvement work process and the meeting notes document showing the list of topics and questions that were linked to Agenda Item G.

- Do a round-robin by teams to get recommended changes, if any, for each of the topics and questions related to Agenda Item G. Add this to the Word document.

- Do an individual round-robin asking for any other recommended changes. Add this to the Word document.

- **Starting question**: "We need to recommend changes to this standard task list for process improvement. We should look back at the issues and topics we want to make sure are covered by our work process. Let's think about any other things we think should be done or not done. Think about ways to improve on the work process and make sure we arrive at what we need. Let's get started."

- Use informed majority to have the team decide changes to the standard work process (Word).

8 min.	H. Team norms

- Have a three-column whiteboard showing a beginning list of team norms and a place to indicate likes and suggestions (whiteboard).

- Give team members five minutes to record what they like and ways to improve.

- Walk through each improvement using informed majority.

- Following the meeting, transfer the agreed-upon items into the meeting notes document (Word).

- **Starting question**: "Think about a team that you have been a part of that worked well. Think about how the team members behaved. Think about the behaviors that contributed to that team being successful. What additions (or changes or deletions) would you recommend to the list of norms that would help us be more like that team?"

- Use informed majority to decide which of the recommendations to use.

12 min.	I. Operating logistics
	• Show the list of decisions the team has to make (Word).
	• What will be our mode of decision making?
	• How often should we meet?
	• When is the best time to meet?
	• What can be communicated to others following each meeting?
	• Use a round robin to request ideas; have people speak for each idea, and use informed majority to make decisions.
	• Record decisions in the meeting document (Word).
5 min.	J. Review and next steps
	• Walk through the meeting notes to show what was done and what was decided.
	• Review the key topics and issues to ensure all were covered.
	• Review any outstanding issues and actions.
	• Remind the group of what can be communicated following the session.
	• Remind the group of next steps and any preparation needed for the next meeting.

5 min.	K. Evaluation and close
	• Have a whiteboard preformatted in two columns "What did you like? What could we do to make future sessions even better?"
	• **Starting question**: "As you reflect on the meeting think about the things that went well, the things that really worked, or the times when the team was productive. As well, think about what could have been done that would have made the meeting even better; consider times when you felt something could have been done differently that would have improved the way things went. Please go ahead and record on the whiteboard in the appropriate area the things you felt went well and the things that would have made the session even better."
	• Review each improvement and type on the whiteboard the number who agree.
	• Following the meeting, copy the evaluation items into the meeting document (Word).
	• Type the information into the meeting document (Word).
	• Hold a summary poll scoring the overall meeting.
Determine meeting rooms, date, and time	You establish a date and time of the meeting. You and the other person in Atlanta agree to be together in a small conference room during the meeting. Since all of the other people are in different locations, there is no need to schedule meeting rooms for them.
Develop and distribute the meeting notice	You prepare a meeting notice and distribute it to all participants. [The meeting notice for this meeting was presented in Chapter 4 and appears as Figure 12.2.] Along with the meeting notice you also distribute the project charge approved by the executive sponsor.

Figure 12.2: Meeting Notice

The Performance Review Improvement Team
xx/xx/xx Gather 8:50 ET / End 11:00 ET 1st Meeting
Be sure to access the link about 10 minutes before the start of the meeting.

Use the following link for the meeting: **www.k1fasf.biz/179avads121**.

If this will be your first time using the virtual meeting platform, please try the link at least twenty-four hours in advance to ensure there are no technical problems. If you need assistance before or during the meeting, contact our moderator, Jim Hamilton, at (770) 555-1440.

Meeting's Purpose
- To kick off the virtual team on improving the performance review process.

Expected Products
- Definition of success, group norms, work process, meetings and logistics plan, communications plan

Proposed Agenda

8:50 Gather

9:00 Start

A. Welcome, charge, deliverables, meeting's purpose

B. Key topics and questions

C. Agenda

D. Ground rules

E. Gifts and hooks

F. Our definition of success

G. Proposed work process

H. Team norms

I. Operating logistics

J. Review and next steps

K. Evaluation and close

11:00 End

Invited Attendees

☐ Kathy K., team leader

☐ Cleve C., documenter   ☐ Ken M.

☐ Bill G.   ☐ Vanessa R

☐ Trina J.   ☐ Andrea T.

In Advance: Review the team charter sent to you last week. Identify any specific meeting issues you would like to see addressed.

Bring to the Meeting: The team charter and your list of issues.

Hold preliminary discussions as needed	You already met with the executive sponsor to fully understand the charge. You decide to hold brief conversations with each team member before the meeting because you have not met most of them.
Prepare the virtual meeting room	The day before the meeting, you prepare the PowerPoint document and the Microsoft Word document that you will use to record information during the virtual meeting.
Select your ground rules	Through your conversations with each team member you recognize you have several highly verbal members on the team who like to tell stories. Accordingly you add a ground rule, "Give end point first" to your list, as follows: • Start and end on time • Everyone speaks • Have one conversation • Use the parking boards • Give end point first • No beeps, buzzes, or ringy-dingies • Meeting work only • Take a stand • Share all relevant information • Explain reasoning and intent • Use the parking boards • Announce yourself when joining/leaving
Prepare your roll call list	You prepare the roll call list for your reference. You'll use it to keep people engaged and not miss anyone during a round-robin. With each process that includes a round-robin, you will start at a different position in the roll call list, but use the same order every time. When someone has spoken, you will check off the person's name and move to the next person in the list. Since, as a team leader, you are also a member of the team, you place your name on the list as well. In some cases you may choose to leave your name off the list if the convention for your meetings is that the team leader only speaks to break ties. The roll call list for the meeting is shown in Figure 12.3 with six columns for checking off names.

Figure 12.3: Roll Call List

						Andrea, Atlanta
						Bill, Boston
						Cleve, Chicago
						Ken, Dallas
						Trina, Denver
						Vanessa, San Diego
						Kathy, Atlanta (project manager)

Prepare your opening words

In the final preparation step, you prepare your opening words to thank, inform, excite, and empower the team, as detailed in the next section.

Starting the Meeting

The agenda for our meeting can be dividing into three stages, as follows:

Starting the Meeting
- Welcome, charge, deliverables, meeting's purpose
- Key topics and questions
- Agenda
- Meeting's ground rules and parking boards
- Gifts and hooks

Running the Meeting
- Our definition of success
- Proposed work process
- Team norms
- Operating logistics

Closing the Meeting
- Review and next steps
- Evaluation and close

This section covers the five agenda items related to starting. In Chapter 5 we describe how the start sets participants' expectations for everything that follows. For our purposes, the start of a meeting includes all the activities done before addressing the first work item on the agenda.

A key step for a successful start is to minimize the impact of technical issues. Accordingly, for this meeting you use the following strategies defined in Chapter 5 to preempt technical issues that could hamper the start.

Strategies to minimize technical issues and their impact

- In the meeting notice you asked people to access the virtual meeting platform at least ten minutes before the meeting begins.

- For those who will be using the virtual meeting platform for the first time, the meeting notice suggested that they test the link at least twenty-four hours in advance to ensure there are no technical problems.

- Because there are more than four other people in the virtual meeting, you assigned someone to serve as the moderator, or technical assistant, whose role it is to resolve any technical issues that you or a participant might have.

- You included the name and telephone number of the moderator in the meeting notice.

- You anticipate needing only ten minutes to set up the virtual meeting room, so you decide to arrive in the physical and virtual meeting room twenty-five minutes before the meeting begins so that you will be ready to go at fifteen minutes before the start. You know that this will give you extra time if you encounter unexpected difficulties.

- When you arrive, you initiate the meeting on your computer and open up, as required, the PowerPoint and Word documents that you will be using.

- You make the title slide of the PowerPoint the opening screen that people will see when they arrive in the virtual meeting room, as shown in Figure 12.4.

Figure 12.4: The Opening Screen

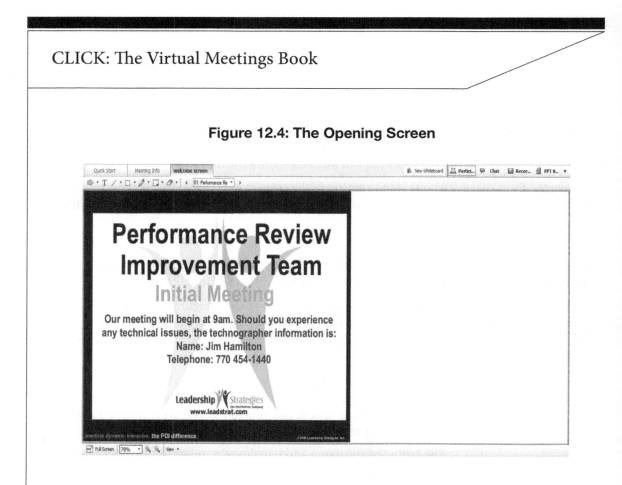

To demonstrate how to get the meeting started, we will walk through the steps you take using the Checklist for Starting, Figure 12.5, which was first presented in Chapter 5.

Figure 12.5: Checklist for Starting

Checklist for Starting

- ❑ Start the meeting on time.
- ❑ Deliver the opening, including purpose and products.*
- ❑ Perform a roll call.*
- ❑ Engage the participants.
- ❑ Confirm the agenda.*
- ❑ Review the ground rules.
- ❑ Review the parking boards.
- ❑ Make introductions, if needed.

* = Recommended for all meetings

Start the meeting on time.	Honoring the request in the meeting notice, people begin arriving in the meeting room about ten minutes before the meeting begins.
A. **Deliver the opening, including purpose and products.**	At 9:00, you start the meeting, speaking with energy and enthusiasm and covering the key parts of an opening statement as described in Chapter 5. *I want to **thank** you all for agreeing to be a part of this meeting.* You show the PowerPoint charge and deliverables slide, Figure 12.6 *Let me start by **informing** you about why we are here.* • *As you all know, we've been having significant difficulty with our performance review process.* • *There have been reports of wide differences among our departments on what is considered "meets" versus "exceeds" versus "far exceeds" expectations. A number of employees have commented that the review process is all about how well you are liked and not how well you perform. Additionally, we have had cases of people being given high ratings just a few months before being fired for poor performance. In summary, it doesn't appear that our performance review process is effective.* • *We have been called together to create a new process that will alleviate concerns like these.* • *When we are done we will have created three items in particular.* You review the deliverables on the slide.

Figure 12.6: Charge and Deliverables

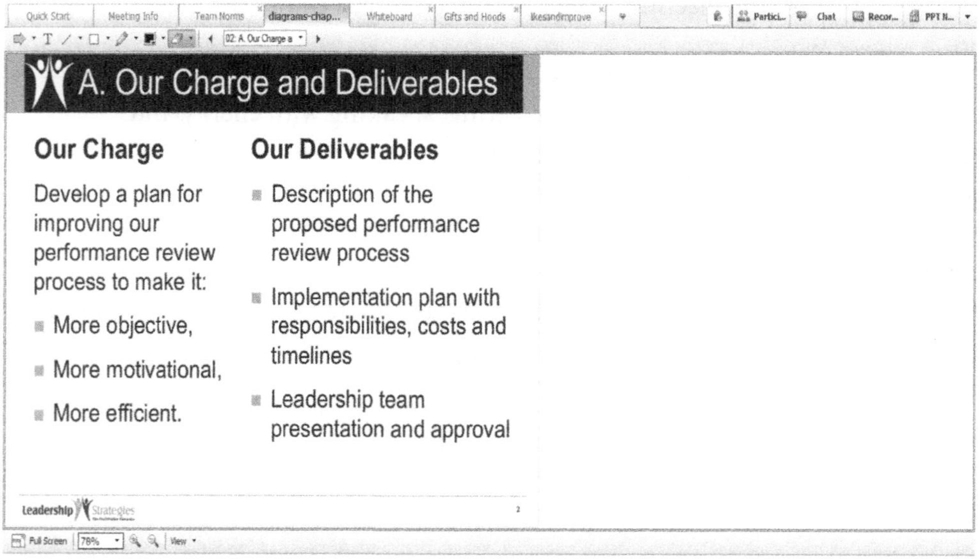

Continue the opening

You continue with the opening by covering the excite portion and today's purpose.

*Why is this **exciting**?*

- *If we are successful, we will have created a process that you and your people can believe in, have faith in, and feel motivated by. And if your people are motivated, you know that it makes your job so much easier: fewer problems, fewer complaints, better morale, and better performance—and a better bottom line means better bonuses for you, me, and everyone in the organization.*

- *In addition, if we do our jobs well, you will have the thanks and gratitude of the senior staff and your peers for the significant improvements you will have made.*

**Continue
the opening**
(continued)

*I want to make sure you know that you have been **empowered** to get this job done.*

- *Each of you was handpicked by your regional vice president to be part of this process.*

- *The VPs believe you have the knowledge as well as the vision for creating a much better process.*

- *And they are looking forward to your recommendations.*

Today's meeting *is about setting the framework for how we will get this work done. Our purpose today is to kick off the virtual team by ensuring that every member is clear on what is to be achieved, how the team is going to achieve it, and the individual roles in making it happen.*

You show the meeting purpose slide, Figure 12.7

Figure 12.7: Meeting Purpose

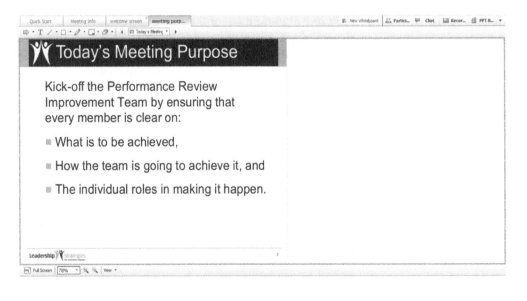

Perform a roll call.

After delivering your opening statement, you perform a roll call by saying the names of the people present on the call and their location and asking them to acknowledge.

> *I would like to do a quick roll call to make sure we all know who is on the call and get used to hearing each other's voices. I'm going to go alphabetically by first name down the list and you can just say something like, "Yes, I'm here." Here we go. Andrea in Atlanta? Bill in Boston? . . .*

> *We'll be using this same alphabetical order at various times during the call when we are wanting to hear from everyone. I will change up the starting point so that Andrea won't have to start every time.*

B.

Engage the participants with Key Topics.

You engage the participants by asking the starting question surrounding key topics and questions.

> *I would like to build a list of the key topics or questions we want to discuss today. I'm going to start with Andrea in Atlanta and go alphabetically down the list. So, think about our charge and deliverables we just went over; imagine the steps we might take in getting it done. Think about the questions you have about what we are being asked to do or how we are going to go about doing it. Think about the ideas you have or the topics you know we need to discuss. Let's build a list. As we start this project, what are the questions or key topics you would like to see discussed? Andrea, get us started."*

You bring up the Word document and record their responses as shown in Figure 12.8. You also make it a point to give yourself a turn during the round-robin and share the topics you want to make sure are discussed.

Figure 12.8: Key Topics

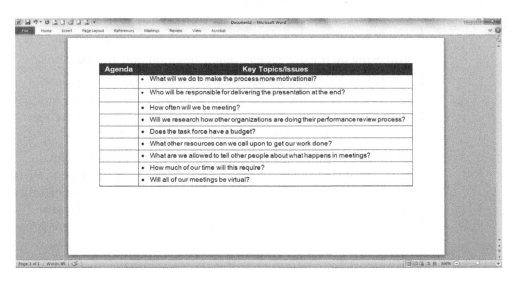

Agenda	Key Topics/Issues
	• What will we do to make the process more motivational?
	• Who will be responsible for delivering the presentation at the end?
	• How often will we be meeting?
	• Will we research how other organizations are doing their performance review process?
	• Does the task force have a budget?
	• What other resources can we call upon to get our work done?
	• What are we allowed to tell other people about what happens in meetings?
	• How much of our time will this require?
	• Will all of our meetings be virtual?

C.

Confirm the agenda.

You do a checkpoint (Chapter 6) and then walk through the agenda and match the topics to be discussed with the agenda item.

Now that we have identified the key topics people want to discuss, I would like to walk through the proposed agenda and see where in the agenda these topics will be covered. This will allow us to determine if we need to change the agenda or defer topics, as needed. So let's review the proposed agenda.

You bring up the PowerPoint agenda slide and explain each agenda item. You then do a split screen to show the agenda slide and the topics recorded earlier in Word.

Now let's go through each of the topics and answer where in the agenda each item will be discussed. To do this, let's work in teams. I would like to have Andrea and Bill on Team 1, Cleve and Trina on Team 2, and Ken and Vanessa on Team 3.

So, Team 1, you are up first. The first topic is, "How will we ensure consistency of rating between supervisors?" Where in our agenda should we discuss this? . . . Great, let's put a "G" next to that item. Team 2, the next item is . . .

After going through all the topics and matching to the agenda, Figure 12.9, you ask the group if changes are needed to the agenda and ask the group to adopt the agenda (as amended) for the session.

Confirm the agenda
(continued)

Now that we have reviewed the agenda and made changes as needed, I would like to make sure we are all in agreement. I am bringing up a poll. You will vote yes or no to adopt the agenda.

You bring up the preloaded agenda adoption poll and execute it.

Let's take a preliminary poll to see if we are ready to adopt the agenda or if more discussion is needed. . . . Based on the results, it appears that we are unanimous in adopting the agenda. Great— we have made our first decision of the meeting.

[Note: A poll may not be necessary in this case, given the few participants in the meeting. You could instead ask for any concerns regarding the agenda. If there are any, you can give the opportunity to those with concerns to share them, along with an alternative recommendation, and then use the consensus building strategies described in Chapter 10.]

Figure 12.9: Key Topics Matched to the Agenda

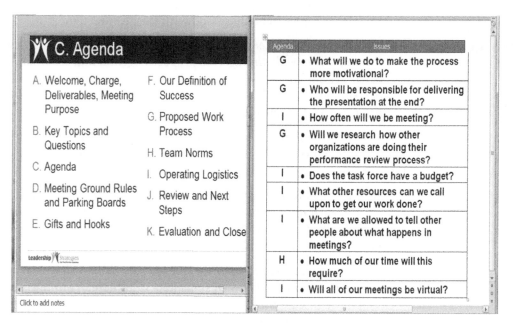

D.

Review the ground rules.

You review the ground rules, get any additions from the group, and ask the group to adopt the ground rules, as well.

Now that we have adopted the agenda, our next step is to define our ground rules for this meeting and future meetings. The ground rules will help us have the same vision for what is needed for us to be interacting effectively during our meetings. I have several ground rules I would like to suggest and then let's add any you think are appropriate. Here is a starting point.

You show the PowerPoint ground rules slide and review each rule. Afterwards you split the screen, as shown in Figure 12.10, to request additions to the ground rules.

Now that I have reviewed the ground rules that I would propose, I would like to get suggestions for any ground rules you would like to add. This time let's start with Bill. Think about meetings you have been in before, either in our organization or others, think about the kinds of behaviors you've seen people do that you think are unproductive or unacceptable; behaviors you want to make sure don't happen within this team. What are additional ground rules you might want to add?

After giving each person an opportunity to add ground rules, ask the group to adopt the ground rules (as amended) for the session using a poll.

Now that we have reviewed the ground rules and suggested additions as needed, I would like to make sure we are all in agreement. I am bringing up a poll. You will vote yes or no to adopt the ground rules.

You bring up the preloaded ground rules adoption poll and execute the poll.

Based on the results, it appears that we are unanimous in adopting the ground rules. Great—we have made our second decision of the meeting.

[Note: As with the agenda, a poll may not be necessary in this case, given the few participants in the meeting.]

Figure 12.10: Ground Rules

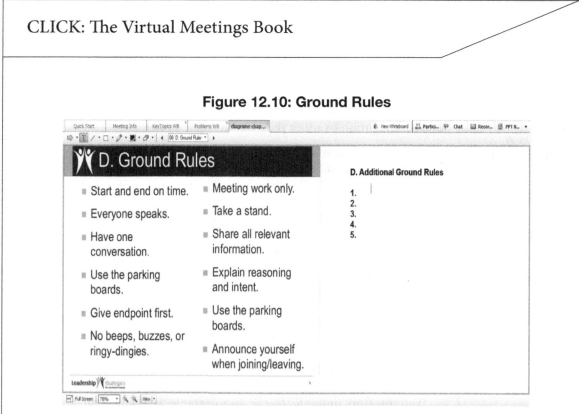

Review the parking boards.	Show the parking boards slide, Figure 12.11.

Throughout our meetings we will be using four parking boards to keep the meeting focused.

- *The issues list is for placing topics that come up that we don't want to discuss at the moment. At the end of each meeting we will clear the issues list by reviewing any items that have been placed on it.*

- *The decisions list is for documenting decisions we make so that we walk out of each meeting with clarity.*

- *The actions list is for defining actions that need to take place outside the meeting. At the end of the meeting we will make sure every action has a person assigned to it, and we'll let that person establish the date by when the action will be completed.*

- *The last parking board is the potential improvement list. During our meetings, when we are talking about how the current process works or the issues with the current process, it is likely that someone will suggest a potential improvement to the process. Instead of waiting until we get to the agenda topic, the potential improvement list is the place to put these ideas. This way, when it's time to talk about how to improve the process we will be able to come back to these ideas easily.*

Figure 12.11: Parking Boards

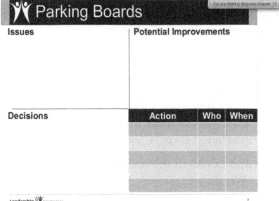

E.

Make introductions if needed using gifts and hooks.

For introductions, you use the gifts and hooks process. You show the gifts and hooks whiteboard, Figure 12.12.

We have just adopted ground rules and gone over the parking boards. The last thing I would like for us to do before we start in on the work is to get to know important information about each of us. I would like to use gifts and hooks to do this.

- *Gifts can be described as what each team member brings to the table that can help the team achieve its objectives. Gifts might be skills, knowledge, experience, resources, connections, etc.*

- *A hook is what has to happen to keep each team member engaged and coming back.*

- *You can see that the whiteboard has a place to record your three gifts and your one hook. You'll have two minutes to do this, and you should type directly onto the whiteboard. Any questions?*

- *So, given our charge and deliverables, each us brings certain gifts to this work, certain skills, experiences, attributes, or resources that will help the team be successful. Think about your gifts. Think about the things that you have that will help the team achieve its goals. In addition, you know what needs to happen to keep you engaged. You know what needs to be*

Make introductions if needed using gifts and hooks.
(continued)

going on that will make you excited about continuing to be a part of the team. What is the most important thing that needs to be going on to keep you hooked? Please record on the whiteboard up to three gifts you bring and one hook."

- *Now that our time is up, I would like to go through the roll call list starting with Cleve this time. I'm going to ask each person to describe his or her gifts and hook. To ensure we don't spend all of our time here, let's limit the description to one minute each. I'll put the timer up so you can see how you are doing. Any questions? Okay, Cleve get us started.*

You will copy the gifts and hooks in the meeting notes document following the meeting (Word).

Figure 12.12: Gifts and Hooks

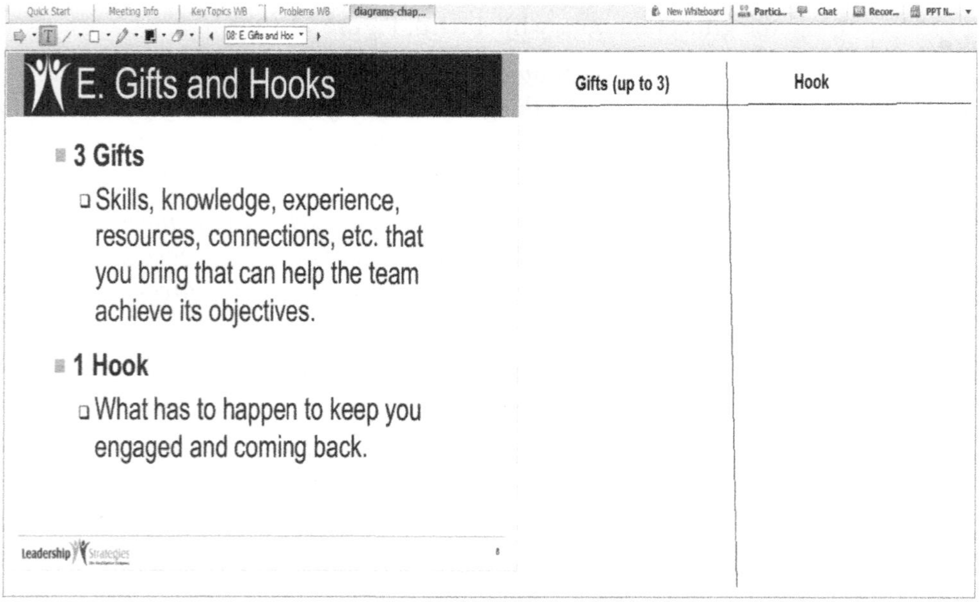

Running the Meeting

While starting the meeting covered the first five agenda items below, running the meeting includes the next four items in the agenda.

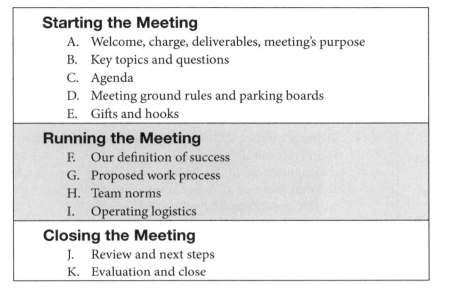

Starting the Meeting
- A. Welcome, charge, deliverables, meeting's purpose
- B. Key topics and questions
- C. Agenda
- D. Meeting ground rules and parking boards
- E. Gifts and hooks

Running the Meeting
- F. Our definition of success
- G. Proposed work process
- H. Team norms
- I. Operating logistics

Closing the Meeting
- J. Review and next steps
- K. Evaluation and close

Chapter 6 describes the steps in running the meeting and summaries the FIRST CLASS approach as summarized in Figure 12.13.

Figure 12.13: Checklist for Running a Meeting

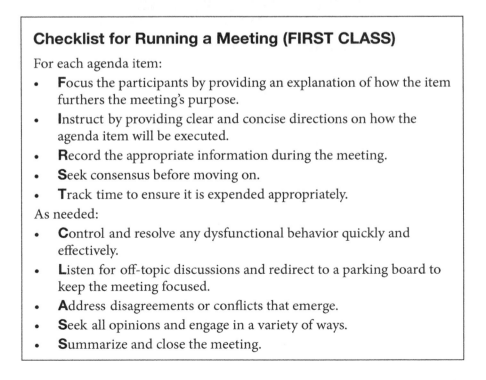

Checklist for Running a Meeting (FIRST CLASS)

For each agenda item:
- **F**ocus the participants by providing an explanation of how the item furthers the meeting's purpose.
- **I**nstruct by providing clear and concise directions on how the agenda item will be executed.
- **R**ecord the appropriate information during the meeting.
- **S**eek consensus before moving on.
- **T**rack time to ensure it is expended appropriately.

As needed:
- **C**ontrol and resolve any dysfunctional behavior quickly and effectively.
- **L**isten for off-topic discussions and redirect to a parking board to keep the meeting focused.
- **A**ddress disagreements or conflicts that emerge.
- **S**eek all opinions and engage in a variety of ways.
- **S**ummarize and close the meeting.

For running the meeting, you will use the FIRST CLASS techniques as you step through the agenda items. For each agenda item, you will start with a checkpoint (review, preview, big view), give directions as appropriate, ask a starting question, and record responses (or get them to record their own if you are using the whiteboard, polling, or chat feature).

F.

Our definition of success

You start by educating the team on measures.

- *We have completed the opening. Let's now get into the work by identifying our definition of success. As Stephen Covey said, it is critical to start with the end in mind. Before we do anything else, let's make sure we all have the same definition of success so that we can cross the finish line together satisfied.*

- *In most projects there are typically three types of measures, as you see on the screen.*

You show the types of measures slide and describe each, Figure 12.14.

Figure 12.14: Types of Measures

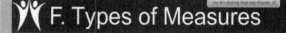

F. Types of Measures

- **Business Outcome Objectives –**
  Reduce the time to process by 50%

- **Project / Process Objectives –**
  Complete project on-time and on-budget

- **Satisfaction Objectives –**
  Have 80% indicate satisfaction or high satisfaction after one year

Leadership Strategies

9

Our definition of success
(continued)

You have the group identify possible measures for the project. You split the screen with the types of measures slide on one screen and the Word document for recording measures and targets on the other.

- *For our project, we want to first decide what yardsticks we should use (the measure), then we will decide where on the yardstick we want to be (the target). So let's do the measures first.*

- *I'm going to start with Ken this time and go through the roll call list. If you have a thought about what we would use as a measure of success, give it to me, I'll list it, and then we'll go on to the next person. If you don't have one, just say, 'Pass.'.*

- *So, let's imagine that we are at the end of the project and it has been a resounding success. How would we know? As we are ending the project, think about the things that would tell us we were successful, that we did a great job. Consider the three categories on the screen. What would tell us we have been successful? Ken, get me started.*

After brainstorming possible measures, you lead the team through informed majority to decide which to use.

- *We have brainstormed the measures. Our next step is to determine which ones are the best ones for us to use so that we can be sure to be measuring only the most important. I would like to use informed majority for this. For each proposed measure I will ask someone to speak for the measure and someone to speak against the measure. If no one speaks for the measure, it will be automatically dropped. If no one speaks against the measure, it will be automatically accepted. If someone speaks for and someone speaks against, I'll ask for other comments and then we'll vote and go with the majority. Will that work for everyone?*

- *Okay, let's get started. The first measure is . . . Would someone speak for it? If not, it goes away. . . . Okay, would someone speak against it? If no one does, it is automatically accepted. . . . Any other comments? Okay, let's vote. . . . Now, let's move on to the next measure.*

After you have the group decide on the measures, you then have them set targets for each, using informed majority once more to resolve differences.

Our definition of success
(continued)

- *Now that we have the yardsticks, the next step is to determine where on the yardstick we want to be. This will set the specific target we will shoot for. Let's use our teams this time and I'll ask Team 2 to recommend a target for the first measure. So imagine that the project is done and we have just completed a full year with the new performance review process. And once more, it's been an amazing success. For this first measure think about the target that would indicate that we have been successful. What is that target?*

- *We have a target recommended. Would someone like to offer a different target? If not, this one is automatically accepted. . . . Any other targets? . . . Okay, now that we have three alternatives we'll have someone speak to each and we'll go with the majority. Let's start with the higher target first . . .*

- *So, it looks like we now have targets for each of our measures.*

Figure 12.15 shows the measures and targets.

Figure 12.15: Measures and Targets

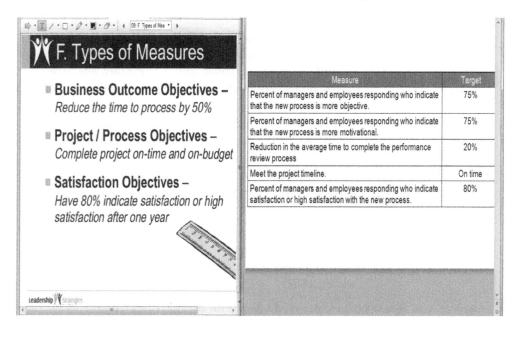

G.
Proposed work process

After giving a checkpoint, you show the standard process improvement work steps (Word) and then create a split screen to check them against the purpose, deliverables, and measures of success.

- *Now that we have decided our measures, our next step is to decide on a work process that ensures we accomplish our purpose, create our deliverables, and achieve our measures of success. This is critical because, before we start on our journey, we need to make sure the roadmap we are following is designed to get us to our desired destination.*

- *Let me walk through the proposed work process . . .*

- *Before we make any improvements to the work process, let's check it against our purpose, deliverables, and measures of success.*

- *I want to start with Team 3 this time. I am pulling up our project's purpose. Is this work process designed to achieve the purpose? . . . The team has said yes. Is there any disagreement from anyone? (If the team says no, you would gather recommendations for improvement.)*

- *Let's go to Team 1. I am pulling up the deliverables. Is this work process designed to create the deliverables?*

- *Now to Team 2. Is the work process designed to achieve our measures of success?*

Figure 12.16 shows the split screen comparing the proposed agenda against the charge and deliverables.

Figure 12.16: Charge and Deliverables versus Proposed Work Process

A. Our Charge and Deliverables	B. Proposed Work Process
Our Charge / **Our Deliverables**	1. How does the process work today?

A. Our Charge and Deliverables

Our Charge

Develop a plan for improving our performance review process to make it:

- More objective,
- More motivational,
- More efficient.

Our Deliverables

- Description of the proposed performance review process
- Implementation plan with responsibilities, costs and timelines
- Leadership team presentation and approval

B. Proposed Work Process

1. How does the process work today?
2. What are the strengths of the current process?
3. What are the problems and root causes?
4. What are the desired performance metrics?
5. What are the critical success factors to achieving these de performance metrics?
6. What are proposed improvements?
7. Which improvements should we implement?
8. What will the new process look like?
9. What are the steps, roles and cost in implementing the nev process?
10. How will we gain approval for this?
    - Steps for developing and distributing the final report
    - Steps for preparing and delivering the presentation
11. What is our evaluation of our results?

Leadership Strategies

Proposed work process
(continued)

Next, you check the work process against the topics and questions collected earlier.

- *We have reviewed the work process against our purpose, deliverables, and measures of success. Now let's review it against the topics and questions collected earlier. This will ensure that our proposed work process will cover these, as well.*

- *Let's focus just on the topics and questions related to Agenda Item G, the work process. I'll start with Team 1 for your recommendation. Team 1, one of the topics we said earlier needed to be covered in the work process is . . . Is that item covered by the work process? If not, what suggestion would you make? . . . Any other comments from any of the other teams?*

- *Okay, let's move on to the next topic or question. Team 2, the item says . . . Is it covered by the work process?*

Finally, you collect any other changes the team would like to make to the work process.

- *I would like to do a quick round-robin starting with Trina this time to see if there are any other changes anyone*

Proposed work process
(continued)

would like to recommend to the work process. During this conversation, there may have been other thoughts you had about how to improve the work process or other suggestions for things to add or subtract. Let's get those out now. Trina, any other suggestions you have? . . . Let's go on to the next person . . .

You use informed majority to process each recommended change.

- *Now that we have all the recommended changes, let's go back through and use informed majority to decide which recommendations to take into account.*

- *The first recommendation is . . . Would someone speak for the recommendation? If no one speaks for it, it goes away as an option. . . . Okay, would someone speak against it? If no one does, it is automatically accepted. . . . Any other comments? Okay, let's vote. . . . Now, let's move on to the next recommendation.*

Figure 12.17 shows the edited and approved work process.

Figure 12.17: Edited and Approved Work Process

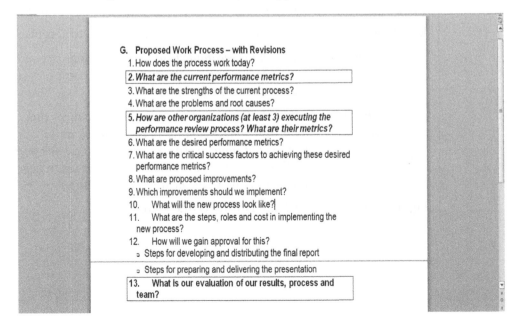

H.

Team norms

Starting with a checkpoint, you bring up the whiteboard of proposed team norms and have the team indicate what they like and recommend changes.

- *We have just confirmed our work process. Our next step is to define our team norms. We have ground rules that define how we operate while in meetings. Team norms focus on how we behave overall. As you will see, these are equally important in helping us achieve success.*

- *I would like to propose the following as a starting point for our norms . . .*

- *Let's take a minute now to type on the whiteboard in the middle column what you like about the norms.*

- *I will quickly read through the likes . . .*

- *Now that we have the likes, let's take three minutes this time to identify any norms you would like to add, change, or delete. You will type these in the right column.*

- *Think about a team that you have been a part of that worked well. Think about how the team members behaved. Think about the behaviors that contributed to that team being successful. What additions (or changes or deletions) would you recommend to the list of norms that would help us be more like that team?*

Use informed majority to decide which recommendations to accept.

- *Now that we have all the recommended changes, let's go back through and use informed majority to decide which recommendations to take into account.*

- *The first recommendation is . . . Would someone speak for the recommendation? If no one speaks for it, it goes away as an option. . . . Okay, would someone speak against it? If no one does, it is automatically accepted. . . Any other comments? Okay, let's vote. . . . Now, let's move on to the next recommendation.*

Figure 12.18 shows the Team Norms Whiteboard.

Figure 12.18: Team Norms Whiteboard

Proposed	Likes	Ways to Improve
▪ We will be prepared for each meeting by reading all materials in advance.		
▪ We will respect one another's time by arriving at least five minutes in advance for all meetings.		
▪ We will fully participate in each meeting.		
▪ We will speak positively of the team and of each other.		

I.

Operating logistics

After a checkpoint, you introduce the four operating logistics decisions (Word).

- *We have defined our Team Norms. Our final major step is to make four decisions about our operating logistics. This will ensure that we are all clear on how we make decisions and what will happen once we leave the virtual meeting. Let's review the decisions we have to make:*

  - *What will be our mode of decision making?*

  - *How often should we meet?*

  - *When is the best time to meet?*

  - *What can be communicated to others following each meeting?*

You then cover the decisions on decision making.

- *Our first operating logistics decision is what our mode for making decisions will be. As you see, I have recommended informed majority for minor decisions, and five-finger consensus for major decisions such as approving a deliverable. Let me explain five-finger consensus . . .*

**Operating
logistics**
(continued)

- *Let's use five-finger consensus to determine if we are fine with my recommended approach for decision making. If you think it's great, give it five fingers, if you agree, give it . . .*

You cover each of the other three decisions using informed majority.

- ### How often should we meet?

  Let's move on to our next operating logistics decision: How often should we meet? Let's get a recommendation from Team 1. Given that we have been asked to complete our work within three months, we could meet weekly, every other week, or monthly. What's your recommendation? Does anyone have an alternative recommendation? Otherwise, we will go with this first one. . . . Now that we have all recommendations, let's have someone speak to each and then call for our vote.

- ### When is the best time to meet?

  Let's move on to our next operating logistics decision: When is the best time to meet? Let's get a recommendation from Team 2. What's your recommendation for the best day and time to meet? Does anyone have an alternative recommendation? Otherwise, we will go with this first one. Now that we have all recommendations, let's have someone speak to each and then call for our vote.

- ### What can be communicated to others following each meeting?

  Let's move on to our next operating logistics decision: What can be communicated to others following each meeting? Let's get a recommendation from Team 3. Given that it will take several meetings for us to complete our work, what's your recommendation about what can be communicated to others following each meeting? Does anyone have an alternative recommendation? Otherwise, we will go with this first one. Now that we have all recommendations, let's have someone speak to each and then call for our vote.

Figure 12.19 shows the operating logistics decisions made.

Figure 12.19: Operating Logistics Decisions

Operating Logistics

What will be our mode of decision-making	5-finger consensus for major decisions; informed majority for minor decisions.
How often should we meet?	Once a week; and possibly daily during the time leading up to the final presentation.
When is the best time to meet?	Thursdays, 11:00 AM-1:00 PM, ET.
What can be communicated to others following each meeting?	Just what we did; no findings, conclusions, recommendations or other commentary.

Closing the Meeting

The final two agenda items cover closing the meeting.

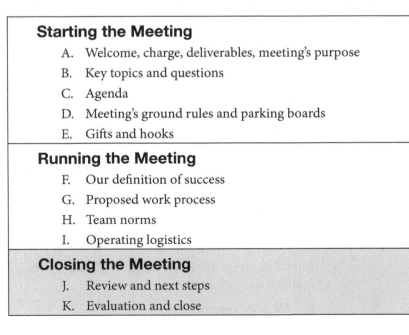

Starting the Meeting

    A.   Welcome, charge, deliverables, meeting's purpose

    B.   Key topics and questions

    C.   Agenda

    D.   Meeting's ground rules and parking boards

    E.   Gifts and hooks

Running the Meeting

    F.   Our definition of success

    G.   Proposed work process

    H.   Team norms

    I.   Operating logistics

Closing the Meeting

    J.   Review and next steps

    K.   Evaluation and close

Chapter 8 describes the eight steps in closing. The eight steps have been divided between our two agenda items, as shown in Figure 12.20.

Figure 12.20: Closing Checklist Breakdown by Agenda Item

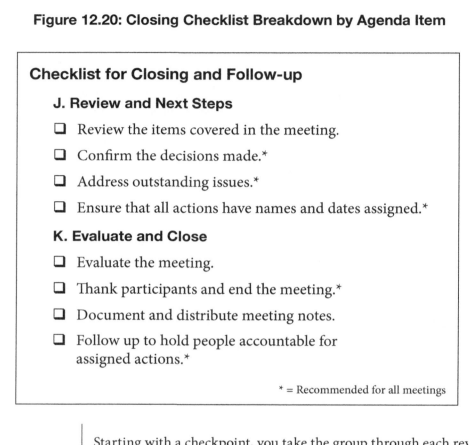

Checklist for Closing and Follow-up

J. Review and Next Steps

❑ Review the items covered in the meeting.

❑ Confirm the decisions made.*

❑ Address outstanding issues.*

❑ Ensure that all actions have names and dates assigned.*

K. Evaluate and Close

❑ Evaluate the meeting.

❑ Thank participants and end the meeting.*

❑ Document and distribute meeting notes.

❑ Follow up to hold people accountable for assigned actions.*

* = Recommended for all meetings

J.

Review and next steps

Starting with a checkpoint, you take the group through each review item and cover next steps. Figure 12.21 gives the closing sequence.

- *We have completed our agenda items and are ready to move into closing. Let's give ourselves a hand!*

- *In closing, let me first walk through the meeting notes to review what was done and what was decided.*

- *Next, let's review the key topics and issues to ensure all were covered. If any were not, stop me and let's discuss what needs to be done.*

- *Next, let's review the issues list so we clear everything off it by asking a series of questions:*

  - *Have we covered it?*

  - *If no, do we need to cover it?*

  - *If yes, do we need to cover it now?*

**Review and
next steps**
(continued)

- *If no, we will move it to the action lists and ask a person to take it on and give a date for when it will be covered.*

- *If yes, it does need to be covered now, and so we will set a time limit and cover it.*

- *Okay, let's look at the first issue . . .*

- *Next, let's review the action lists to define what will happen when we leave the room, add any additional actions, and assign a person to each who will then give us a date by when the action will be completed.*

- *Next, I want to remind everyone of what we said can be communicated following the session.*

- *Finally, let's talk about any immediate next steps and any preparation needed for the next meeting.*

Figure 12.21: The Closing Sequence

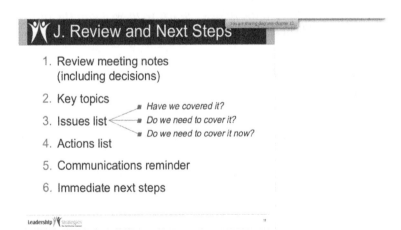

J. Review and Next Steps

1. Review meeting notes
   (including decisions)

2. Key topics

3. Issues list
   - Have we covered it?
   - Do we need to cover it?
   - Do we need to cover it now?

4. Actions list

5. Communications reminder

6. Immediate next steps

Leadership Strategies

K.
Evaluation and close

Following a checkpoint, you show a whiteboard preformatted in two columns and ask the participants to fill in each: "What did you like? What could we do to make future sessions even better?"

- *Now that we have completed the meeting, I would like for us to take a second to focus on what went well during the meeting and ways the session could have been better. This will help make our future meetings even more productive.*

- *I am putting up a whiteboard now with two columns. On the left I would like for you to type in the things that went well during the meeting. On the right please indicate ways to make the meeting even better next time. We will have four minutes to do this.*

- *As you reflect on the meeting, think about the things that went well, the things that really worked, or the times when the team was very productive. Also think about what could have been done that would have made the meeting even better; consider times when you felt something could have been done differently that would have improved the way things went. Please go ahead and record on the whiteboard in the appropriate area the things you felt went well and the things that will help make future sessions even better.*

You review with the group what was said and have the team make decisions about the improvement recommendations using informed majority.

- *Let's review what people said they liked about the meeting.*

- *Now, let's go back and review each of the improvement suggestions. While maybe only one person mentioned it, we need to decide as a group if we want to implement this recommendation. Let's go through them one at a time and use the informed majority process.*

- *The first recommendation is . . . Would someone speak for the recommendation? If no one speaks for it, it goes away as an option. . . . Okay, would someone speak against it? If no one does, it is automatically accepted. . . . Any other comments? Okay, let's vote. . . . Now, let's move on to the next recommendation.*

Evaluation and close
(continued)

You hold a summary poll scoring the overall meeting.

- *To summarize how well this meeting went, let's do a summary poll scoring the meeting on a 0-to-10 scale with 10 being most favorable. How would you rate this meeting? Enter your score now.*

- *Let's look at the results.*

You thank everyone and end the meeting.

- *Any other comments from anyone before we close the meeting?*

- *Well, thanks everyone for a fantastic meeting. I'll be getting the meeting notes out within two business days. Our next meeting is . . . I will talk with you all then.*

Following the meeting, you copy the evaluation items into the meeting document (Word).

Figure 12.22 shows the evaluation whiteboard

Figure 12.22: The Evaluation Whiteboard

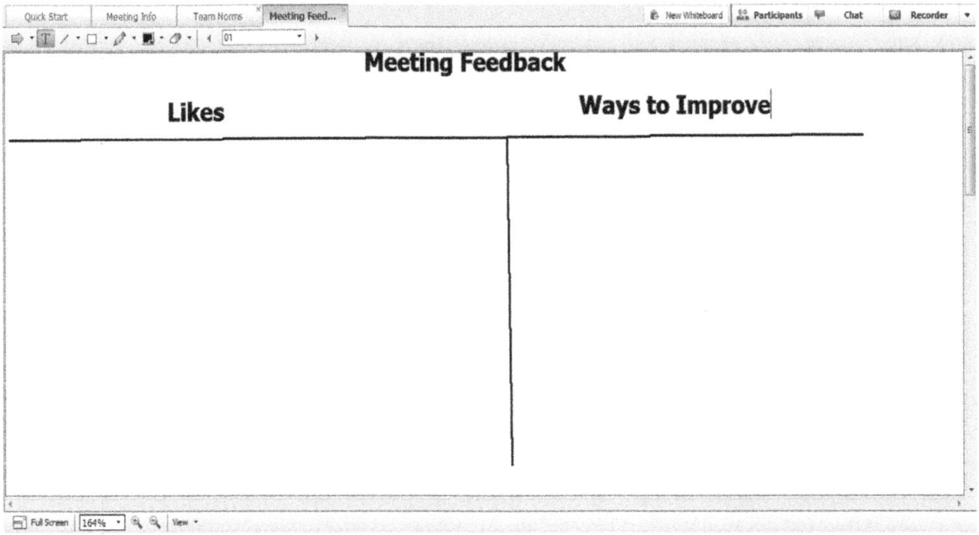

A Final Word

We hope this detailed look inside a virtual meeting has left you with several key impressions.

- A highly engaging, highly effective virtual meeting requires significant planning and preparation.

- The use of facilitation techniques like checkpoints, starting questions, and informed majority serves to create a highly interactive and productive virtual meeting environment.

- The virtual meetings platform can be used as an effective tool for varying engagement approaches.

- You can indeed have masterful virtual meetings that lead to better results with significantly higher levels of buy-in and commitment to action.

Now that you have completed this book, please take the next step by putting these strategies into practice. With your next meeting, use the checklist for preparing to ensure you plan for a successful virtual session. Begin the meeting with focus and high engagement by employing the checklist for starting. Run the meeting effectively using the FIRSTCLASS steps. Close the meeting and follow-up as defined by the closing checklist. Employ these strategies and you can expect your participants to give you rave reviews.

Our hope is that this book will be a catalyst for you in achieving amazing results in your virtual meetings.

Strategies List

The sixty strategies discussed in *CLICK: The Virtual Meetings Book* are listed below.

Strategy 1.   Ensure that your team understands the common problems with virtual and face-to-face meetings and the unique problems with virtual meetings.

Strategy 2.   Establish a vision of a masterful virtual meeting that addresses both the common and the unique problems.

Strategy 3.   Define and communicate the role of virtual meeting leaders and the role of virtual meeting participants.

Strategy 4.   Educate meeting leaders and participants on the different meeting types, their differences, and when each is appropriate.

Strategy 5.   Equip meeting leaders and participants with the questions to ask for determining if a meeting is really necessary and for eliminating unnecessary ones.

Strategy 6.   Assess which meetings can be conducted virtually versus face to face and document the cost savings associated with conducting virtual meetings.

Strategy 7.   Find out why the organization is moving to virtual and what is needed, being sure to identify specific budget constraints and other requirements.

Strategy 8.   View a variety of platforms to gain an understanding of features.

Strategy 9.   Determine your critical three to seven features needed.

Strategy 10.   Narrow your choices to the product tier for your critical features.

Strategy 11.   Select the virtual meeting platform that best meets your needs and constraints.

Strategy 12.   For your meeting, define the six Ps of preparation: purpose, products, participants, probable issues, process, and platform.

Strategy 13.   Design an agenda to achieve the purpose and products, taking into account the participants and probable issues.

Strategy 14.   Prepare a detailed agenda that describes how you will use the virtual meeting platform to execute each agenda item.

Strategy 15.   Use a variety of information gathering processes to make the meeting interesting and engaging.

Strategy 16.   Distribute a meeting notice in advance of the meeting to notify participants of the meeting's purpose and the virtual meeting access link, and to encourage participants to prepare for the meeting.

Strategy 17.   Be sure that the first time appearing on the meeting notice is the gathering time—not the start time.

Strategy 18.   Hold preliminary discussions with people if the meeting is critical or includes controversial topics.

Strategy 19.   Ask people to access the virtual meeting platform at least ten minutes before the meeting is supposed to start.

Strategy 20.   If you are expecting more than three or four other people in the virtual meeting, assign someone not participating in the meeting to serve as the moderator, or technical assistant, whose role it is to be the point of contact for resolving any technical issues that you or a participant might have.

Strategy 21.   Achieve an on-time start by making the first time on the agenda the gathering time and gaining advance permission to start on time.

Strategy 22.   Deliver a strong, effective opening by:

- thanking the participants for coming,

- informing them of the purpose and desired products,

- exciting them about the benefits to them, and

- empowering them by identifying the authority they have been given and role they play.

Strategy 23.   To ensure that you are aware of everyone who is on the call and to allow people to begin connecting voices to names, perform a roll call with names and location, and ask each person to acknowledge with a, "Yes, I'm here."

Strategy 24.   For each location with multiple people, assign a person as your "eyes in the room" to alert you when you need to slow down, speed up, or take an alternative action based on what is happening in the room.

Strategy 25.   Get the participants engaged early in the meeting by using a visual starting question focused on key topics, personal outcomes, one-minute check-ins, or any other subject appropriate for the meeting.

Strategy 26.   Gain buy-in to the agenda by linking the participants' personal outcomes or key topics to the agenda.

Strategy 27.   Use ground rules to identify in-bounds and out-of-bounds behavior.

Strategy 28.   Establish parking boards to have a place to "park" decisions made, actions to be taken, or issues to be addressed at a later time.

Strategy 29.   To get everyone on the same page and achieve a smooth flow through the agenda, take a checkpoint at the beginning of every agenda item.

- Review quickly what has been done to date.

- Describe briefly what the group is about to do.

- Explain how the previewed agenda item fits into the meeting's overall purpose.

Strategy 30.   When giving directions, describe what to do, how to do it, and why doing it is important. Use the PeDeQs format.

- Give the overall **P**urpose of the activity.

- When appropriate, use a simple **E**xample that is outside the topic area.

- Give general **D**irections using verbal pictures.

- Give specific **E**xceptions and special cases.

- Ask for **Q**uestions.

- Ask a **S**tarting Question that gets participants visualizing the answers.

Strategy 31.   Record all key information provided during the meeting, including all issues, decisions, actions, and relevant analysis for future reference. Be sure to record the information without personal bias.

Strategy 32.   Use a virtual meeting platform that permits everyone to see the recorded comments. Where appropriate, have the participants record their own responses rather than your doing it for them.

Strategy 33.   Before moving on to the next agenda item, summarize the information covered and use a round-robin to ask the participants, "Can we move on?"

Strategy 34.   Track time against your plan to ensure that the meeting time is spent in the most appropriate way.

Strategy 35.   If the group begins to detour, bring the group back by asking a redirection question, "That's an interesting point. Can we put that on the issues list so we don't forget it, and then get back to our question?"

Strategy 36.   Seek all opinions and engage in a variety of ways, including round-robins, whips, polls, whiteboards, and breakout groups.

Strategy 37.   For each agenda item in the virtual meeting, use the appropriate process based on the purpose of the agenda item.

Strategy 38.   To generate ideas, use brainstorming.

Strategy 39.   To create a list of details, use listing.

Strategy 40.   To categorize information, use grouping.

Strategy 41.   To identify items of most importance, use prioritizing.

Strategy 42.   To collect opinions and input, use feedback or polling.

Strategy 43.   To gain rapid feedback, use the whip.

Strategy 44.   To increase participation and efficiency, use breakouts.

Strategy 45.   To identify and respond to specific questions, use Q-and-A.

Strategy 46. To gain a response from everyone, use a round-robin.

Strategy 47. Before closing the meeting, thoroughly review the following:

- The agenda and all items covered in the meeting and any key topics or participant outcomes identified at the start

- The decisions made by the team, documenting benefits if necessary

- Any open issues in order to determine what action, if any, is needed on them

- All actions to ensure that a person and a date are assigned to each

Strategy 48. Use a brief process of identifying strengths, improvements, and a rating for the meeting to gain valuable feedback on how to improve future meetings.

Strategy 49. To maintain clarity around decisions made and actions to be taken as a result of the meeting, distribute a summary following the meeting that includes decisions, actions, open issues, and relevant analysis documented during the meeting.

Strategy 50. To help ensure that actions assigned during the meeting are accomplished, distribute a notice highlighting actions to be completed several days before the next meeting. Additionally, in the next meeting, include a review of prior actions as the first or second agenda item.

Strategy 51. Understand the typical dysfunctions that can afflict virtual meetings so that you will be prepared with prevention and response strategies, should the need arise.

Strategy 52. In general, when responding to dysfunction,

- approach privately or generally,

- empathize with the symptom,

- address the root cause, and

- get agreement on the solution.

Strategy 53. Early on, decide how decisions will be made.

Strategy 54. Use five-finger consensus as a decision-making vehicle to gain a broad base of agreement without jeopardizing the quality of a solution, as often happens when unanimous support is sought.

Strategy 55. Use informed majority for less significant decisions to help ensure relevant information is discussed.

Strategy 56. When faced with a disagreement, determine whether the disagreement is Level 1 (information), 2 (values or experience), or 3 (personality, past history, or other outside factors).

Strategy 57. Apply the appropriate consensus building strategy—delineation, strengths-weaknesses-merging, or higher source—depending on the level of the disagreement.

Strategy 58. If only a few people are remote, use the ground rule, "Don't lose the remote," and be sure to include remote participants throughout the meeting by starting with them first.

Strategy 59. If a large number of people are remote, divide the group into teams; use round-robins by team; ask every member of half or fewer of the teams to specifically respond in each activity.

Strategy 60. If you are the only person not in the room, choose a virtual meeting platform that allows for video, assign someone to serve as your eyes in the room, and consider webcams at every table so you can observe the interaction.

Michael Wilkinson

Michael Wilkinson is the managing director of Leadership Strategies—The Facilitation Company, an organization that specializes in training in facilitation, consulting, leadership, and meeting skills. Leadership Strategies also provides professional facilitators around the world to help organizations with strategic planning, issue resolution, focus groups, and a variety of other processes.

Michael is a leader in the facilitation industry. He is the author of the industry best-seller, **The Secrets of Facilitation**, and also **The Secrets to Masterful Meetings**, **The Executive Guide to Facilitating Strategy**, and **Buying Styles**. He is the founder of the FindaFacilitator Database, serves on the board of the International Institute for Facilitation, and led the creation of the International Facilitation Impact Awards. He was one of the first five Certified Professional Facilitators in North America and has been subsequently awarded the prestigious Certified *Master* Facilitator designation. In 2003, the Southeast Association of Facilitators named him Facilitator of the Year for his achievements and contributions to the field.

He is a much-sought-after facilitator, trainer, and speaker, nationally as well as internationally. He has completed international assignments in Bangkok, Brisbane, Geneva, Glasgow, Hamburg, Helsinki, Hong Kong, Istanbul, London, Melbourne, Milan, the Netherlands, Oxford, Saudi Arabia, Singapore, Sydney, and Wellington. He has worked with hundreds of public and private sector organizations, including The Coca-Cola Company, KPMG Peat Marwick, the Centers for Disease Control, and the United Way Worldwide.

Prior to founding Leadership Strategies, he was a Senior Manager in Ernst & Young's Management Consulting Group. As an accomplished information technology consultant, he was selected by the governor of his state to serve for two terms on the governor's twelve-member Information Technology Policy Council.

Michael resides in Atlanta with his wife and two children.

Richard Smith

Richard is a principal with Leadership Strategies and leads the training and facilitation services division. He is responsible for the twenty-plus members of the organization's core facilitation team and the 500-plus facilitators under contract through the firm's FindaFacilitator.com network. Richard specializes in certifying core team members and clients on the firm's flagship course, "The Effective Facilitator," as well as other courses. Richard is a Certified *Master* Facilitator, one of fewer than thirty in the world.

Prior to Leadership Strategies, Richard was an executive with software services companies where he had responsibility for the delivery, training, and support of complex systems including customer relationship management, finance, human resources, and enterprise requirements planning. In these roles Richard had in-depth experience facilitating sessions with clients, vendors, partners, and staff in the design, implementation, and support of mission-critical projects. In these roles he led the training of over ten thousand professionals and administrative support personnel. His roles included those of executive vice president of services, chief operating officer, and chief executive officer. Earlier in his career, Richard was a consultant with Andersen Consulting (now Accenture) for over eight years, where he worked on engagements in the area of strategic planning, profit improvement, change management, and systems development. He was part of the team that developed the firm's training materials for facilitation and leadership programs as well as project management.

Richard has worked with large clients including the Southern Company, Coca-Cola, Georgia Power, Novartis, M&M Mars, many federal and state government agencies, and several early-stage companies.

Richard received his BS from the U. S. Naval Academy in Annapolis, Maryland and his MBA from The Ohio State University. While with Andersen, he earned his CPA in the State of Georgia. Richard is married and has two daughters and four grandchildren.

About Leadership Strategies

In 1992, Leadership Strategies, Inc. (LSI) was established to provide two things: facilitation training and meeting facilitation services. Today, the company continues its practice as the leading facilitation company in the nation with over 18,000 trained graduates and over 500 professional facilitators in its network. Based in Atlanta, Georgia, LSI offers both its training and its facilitation services worldwide to commercial, government, and non-profit organizations.

When it comes to training, we "facili-train"! Unlike most instructor-led courses that offer minimal opportunities for practice and feedback, when you take a course from LSI, over 50 percent of the class will be practice sessions, role-plays, group interactions, or highly engaging team exercises.

Our Virtual Meeting Facilitation Training

The more people in an organization who are skilled at leading effective virtual meetings, the more capable an organization is of managing teams, leading people virtually, creating strategy, and getting results.

Rather than having training courses that focus pri on virtual tool training, we focus on facilitation skills for the virtual environment. We offer two courses in which you'll learn how to combine technology with facilitation methods to increase productivity and ensure your virtual meetings are highly engaging and highly productive.

Our *Facilitating Virtual Meetings—Essentials* course is designed for any professional who leads virtual meetings in which all or a portion of the team members, clients, vendors, contractors, and other meeting participants are offsite. In it you'll learn how to do the following:

- Prepare your virtual meeting place
- Determine the meeting's purpose and products
- Develop an agenda that achieves the purpose
- Use the virtual tool to facilitate high levels of interaction
- Effectively manage dysfunction and disagreements
- Maintain high energy
- Build consensus
- Keep remote participants engaged, focused, and involved
- Reduce or eliminate multitasking
- And more

Our *Facilitating Virtual Meetings—Comprehensive* course is for people who lead complex virtual meetings or whose success requires having expertise in facilitating virtual groups. Along with covering the essentials described above, this course delivers a wealth of engagement strategies and practice sessions. Participants walk away with the confidence that they can deliver more effective virtual meetings because they have seen it done and have done it themselves during the training session.

If you are interested in Facilitating Virtual Meetings training for your team, contact us by telephone, through our website, or by e-mail. You can also subscribe to our free newsletter, *Leaders Digest*, or take advantage of one of our free webinars.

Leadership Strategies
The Facilitation Company

www.leadstrat.com   800-824-2850   info@leadstrat.com

Bibliography

Barlow, J. *Smart Videoconferencing: New Habits for Virtual Meetings*. San Francisco: Berrett-Koehler Publishers, 2002.

Bens, I. *Facilitating with Ease! Core Skills for Facilitators, Team Leaders and Members, Managers, Consultants, and Trainers* (3rd ed.). San Francisco: Jossey-Bass, 2012.

Courville, R. *102 Tips for Online Meetings*. Seattle: CreateSpace Independent Publishing Platform, 2013

Doyle, M., and Straus, D. *How to Make Meetings Work! The New Interaction Method*. New York: Berkley Books, 1976.

Hunter, D. *The Art of Facilitation: The Essentials for Leading Great Meetings and Creating Group Synergy*. San Francisco: Jossey-Bass, 2009.

Kaner, S., and others. *Facilitator's Guide to Participatory Decision-Making*. Philadelphia: New Society, 1996.

Koegel, T. *The Exceptional Presenter Goes Virtual: Take Command of Your Message, Create an "In-Person" Experience, and Captivate Any Remote Audience*. Austin: Greenleaf Book Group Press, 2010.

Rees, F. *How to Lead Work Teams: Facilitation Skills*. (2nd ed.). San Francisco: Jossey-Bass, 2001.

Schwarz, R. *The Skilled Facilitator: A Comprehensive Resource for Consultants, Facilitators, Managers, Trainers, and Coaches*. San Francisco: Jossey-Bass, 2002.

Settle-Murphy, N. *Leading Effective Virtual Teams: Overcoming Time and Distance to Achieve Exceptional Results*. Boca Raton: Auerbach Publications, 2012.

Sookman, C. *Effective Virtual Meetings: Tips for Teleconference and Webinar Leaders*. Oshawa, Ontario: Multi-Media Publications Inc., 2009.

Weaver, R., and Farrell, J. *Managers as Facilitators: A Practical Guide to Getting Work Done in a Changing Workplace*. San Francisco: Berrett-Koehler, 1997.

Wilkinson, M. *The Executive Guide to Facilitating Strategy*. Atlanta: Leadership Strategies Publishing, 2011.

Wilkinson, M. *The Secrets of Facilitation-New and Revised*. San Francisco: Jossey-Bass, 2012.

Wilkinson, M. *The Secrets to Masterful Meetings*. Atlanta: Leadership Strategies Publishing, 2005.

References

1   Adapted from Michael Wilkinson, *The Secrets to Masterful Meetings: Ignite a Meetings Revolution*. (Atlanta: Leadership Strategies Publishing, 2005), 5.

2   Michael Wilkinson, *The Secrets of Facilitation-New and Revised*. (San Francisco: Jossey-Bass, 2012).

3   Michael Wilkinson, *The Secrets to Masterful Meetings: Ignite a Meetings Revolution*. (Atlanta: Leadership Strategies Publishing, 2005), 9.

4   Ibid., 27.

5   Adapted from *The Skilled Facilitator: A Comprehensive Resource for Consultants, Facilitators, Managers, Trainers, and Coaches (New and Revised)* by Roger Schwarz. San Francisco: Jossey-Bass, 2002.

6   Ibid.

7   Ibid.

8   Michael Wilkinson, *The Secrets of Facilitation-New and Revised*. (San Francisco: Jossey-Bass, 2012), 21.

9   Michael Wilkinson, *The Secrets to Masterful Meetings: Ignite a Meetings Revolution*. (Atlanta: Leadership Strategies Publishing, 2005), 46.

10   Ibid., 52.

11   Ibid., 53.

12   Adapted from Michael Wilkinson, *The Secrets of Facilitation-New and Revised*. (San Francisco: Jossey-Bass, 2012) Chapter 7, 123.

13   Ibid., 178.

14   Adapted from Michael Wilkinson, *The Secrets to Masterful Meetings: Ignite a Meetings Revolution*. (Atlanta: Leadership Strategies Publishing, 2005), Chapter 8, 92.

15   Ibid., 111.

16   Adapted from Michael Wilkinson, *The Secrets of Facilitation-New and Revised*. (San Francisco: Jossey-Bass, 2012) Chapter 13, 287.

17   Ibid, 282.

CPSIA information can be obtained at www.ICGtesting.com
Printed in the USA
BVOW10s1800040614

355400BV00005B/158/P